The Ver

Fannie Hurst

Alpha Editions

This edition published in 2024

ISBN : 9789362920324

Design and Setting By
Alpha Editions
www.alphaedis.com
Email - info@alphaedis.com

Contents

SHE WALKS IN BEAUTY

By that same architectural gesture of grief which caused Jehan at Agra to erect the Taj Mahal in memory of a dead wife and a cold hearthstone, so the Bon Ton hotel, even to the pillars with red-freckled monoliths and peacock-backed lobby chairs, making the analogy rather absurdly complete, reared its fourteen stories of "elegantly furnished suites, all the comforts and none of the discomforts of home."

A mausoleum to the hearth. And as true to form as any that ever mourned the dynastic bones of an Augustus or a Hadrian.

An Indiana-limestone and Vermont-marble tomb to Hestia.

All ye who enter here, at sixty dollars a week and up, leave behind the lingo of the fireside chair, parsley bed, servant problem, cretonne shoe bags, hose nozzle, striped awnings, attic trunks, bird houses, ice-cream salt, spare-room matting, bungalow aprons, mayonnaise receipt, fruit jars, spring painting, summer covers, fall cleaning, winter apples.

The mosaic tablet of the family hotel is nailed to the room side of each door and its commandments read something like this:

One ring: Bell Boy.

Two rings: Chambermaid.

Three rings: Valet.

Under no conditions are guests permitted to use electric irons in rooms.

Cooking in rooms not permitted.

No dogs allowed.

Management not responsible for loss or theft of jewels. Same can be deposited for safe-keeping in the safe at office.

* * * * *

Note:

Our famous two-dollar Table d'Hôte dinner is served in the Red Dining Room from six-thirty to eight. Music.

It is doubtful if in all its hothouse garden of women the Hotel Bon Ton boasted a broken finger nail or that little brash place along the forefinger that tattles so of potato peeling or asparagus scraping.

- 1 -

The fourteenth-story manicure, steam bath, and beauty parlors saw to all that. In spite of long bridge table, lobby divan, and table-d'hôte séances, "tea" where the coffee was served with whipped cream and the tarts built in four tiers and mortared in mocha filling, the Bon Ton hotel was scarcely more than an average of fourteen pounds overweight.

Forty's silhouette, except for that cruel and irrefutable place where the throat will wattle, was almost interchangeable with eighteen's. Indeed, Bon Ton grandmothers with backs and French heels that were twenty years younger than their throats and bunions, vied with twenty's profile.

Whistler's kind of mother, full of sweet years that were richer because she had dwelt in them, but whose eyelids were a little weary, had no place there.

Mrs. Gronauer, who occupied an outside, southern-exposure suite of five rooms and three baths, jazzed on the same cabaret floor with her granddaughters.

Many the Bon Ton afternoon devoted entirely to the possible lack of length of the new season's skirts or the intricacies of the new filet-lace patterns.

Fads for the latest personal accoutrements gripped the Bon Ton in seasonal epidemics.

The permanent wave swept it like a tidal one.

In one winter of afternoons enough colored-silk sweaters were knitted in the lobby alone to supply an orphan asylum, but didn't.

The beaded bag, cunningly contrived, needleful by needleful, from little strands of colored-glass caviar, glittered its hour.

Filet lace came then, sheerly, whole yokes of it for crêpe-de-Chine nightgowns and dainty scalloped edges for camisoles.

Mrs. Samstag made six of the nightgowns that winter—three for herself and three for her daughter. Peach-blowy pink ones with lace yokes that were scarcely more to the skin than the print of a wave edge running up sand, and then little frills of pink-satin ribbon, caught up here and there with the most delightful and unconvincing little blue-satin rosebuds.

It was bad for her neuralgic eye, the meanderings of the filet pattern, but she liked the delicate threadiness of the handiwork, and Mr. Latz liked watching her.

There you have it! Straight through the lacy mesh of the filet to the heart interest.

Mr. Louis Latz, who was too short, slightly too stout, and too shy of likely length of swimming arm ever to have figured in any woman's inevitable visualization of her ultimate Leander, liked, fascinatedly, to watch Mrs. Samstag's nicely manicured fingers at work. He liked them passive, too. Best of all, he would have preferred to feel them between his own, but that had never been.

Nevertheless, that desire was capable of catching him unawares. That very morning as he had stood, in his sumptuous bachelor's apartment, strumming on one of the windows that overlooked an expansive tree-and-lake vista of Central Park, he had wanted very suddenly and very badly to feel those fingers in his and to kiss down on them.

Even in his busy broker's office, this desire could cut him like a swift lance.

He liked their taper and their rosy pointedness, those fingers, and the dry, neat way they had of stepping in between the threads.

Mr. Latz's nails were manicured, too, not quite so pointedly, but just as correctly as Mrs. Samstag's. But his fingers were stubby and short. Sometimes he pulled at them until they cracked.

Secretly he yearned for length of limb, of torso, even of finger.

On this, one of a hundred such typical evenings in the Bon Ton lobby, Mr. Latz, sighing out a satisfaction of his inner man, sat himself down on a red-velvet chair opposite Mrs. Samstag. His knees, widespread, taxed his knife-pressed gray trousers to their very last capacity, but he sat back in none the less evident comfort, building his fingers up into a little chapel.

"Well, how's Mr. Latz this evening?" asked Mrs. Samstag, her smile encompassing the question.

"If I was any better I couldn't stand it," relishing her smile and his reply.

The Bon Ton had just dined, too well, from fruit flip *à la* Bon Ton, mulligatawny soup, filet of sole *sauté*, choice of or both *poulette emincé* and spring lamb *grignon*, and on through to fresh strawberry ice cream in fluted paper boxes, *petits fours*, and *demi-tasse*. Groups of carefully corseted women stood now beside the invitational plush divans and peacock chairs, paying twenty minutes' after-dinner standing penance. Men with Wall Street eyes and blood pressure slid surreptitious celluloid toothpicks and gathered around the cigar stand. Orchestra music flickered. Young girls, the traditions of demure sixteen hanging by one-inch shoulder straps, and who could not walk across a hardwood floor without sliding the last three steps, teetered in bare arm-in-arm groups, swapping persiflage with pimply, patent-leather-haired young men who were full of nervous excitement and eager to excel in return badinage.

Bell hops scurried with folding tables. Bridge games formed.

The theater group got off, so to speak. Showy women and show-off men. Mrs. Gronauer, in a full-length mink coat that enveloped her like a squaw, a titillation of diamond aigrettes in her Titianed hair, and an aftermath of scent as tangible as the trail of a wounded shark, emerged from the elevator with her son and daughter-in-law.

"Foi!" said Mr. Latz, by way of somewhat unduly, perhaps, expressing his own kind of cognizance of the scented trail.

"*Fleur de printemps*," said Mrs. Samstag, in quick olfactory analysis. "Eight-ninety-eight an ounce." Her nose crawling up to what he thought the cunning perfection of a sniff.

"Used to it from home—not? She is not. Believe me, I knew Max Gronauer when he first started in the produce business in Jersey City and the only perfume he had was at seventeen cents a pound and not always fresh killed at that. *Cold storage de printemps!*"

"Max Gronauer died just two months after my husband," said Mrs. Samstag, tucking away into her beaded handbag her filet-lace handkerchief, itself guilty of a not inexpensive attar.

"Thu-thu!" clucked Mr. Latz for want of a fitting retort.

"Heigh-ho! I always say we have so little in common, me and Mrs. Gronauer, she revokes so in bridge, and I think it's terrible for a grandmother to blondine so red, but we've both been widows for almost eight years. Eight years," repeated Mrs. Samstag on a small, scented sigh.

He was inordinately sensitive to these allusions, reddening and wanting to seem appropriate.

"Poor little woman, you've had your share of trouble."

"Share," she repeated, swallowing a gulp and pressing the line of her eyebrows as if her thoughts were sobbing. "I—It's as I tell Alma, Mr. Latz, sometimes I think I've had three times my share. My one consolation is that I try to make the best of it. That's my motto in life, 'Keep a bold front.'"

For the life of him, all he could find to convey to her the bleeding quality of his sympathy was, "Poor, poor little woman!"

"Heigh-ho!" she said, and again, "Heigh-ho!"

There was quite a nape to her neck. He could see it where the carefully trimmed brown hair left it for a rise to skillful coiffure, and what threatened to be a slight depth of flesh across the shoulders had been carefully massaged of this tendency, fifteen minutes each night and morning, by her daughter.

In fact, through the black transparency of her waist Mr. Latz thought her plumply adorable.

It was about the eyes that Mrs. Samstag showed most plainly whatever inroads into her clay the years might have gained. There were little dark areas beneath them like smeared charcoal, and two unrelenting sacs that threatened to become pouchy.

Their effect was not so much one of years, but they gave Mrs. Samstag, in spite of the only slightly plump and really passable figure, the look of one out of health. Women of her kind of sallowness can be found daily in fashionable physicians' outer offices, awaiting X-ray appointments.

What ailed Mrs. Samstag was hardly organic. She was the victim of periodic and raging neuralgic fires that could sweep the right side of her head and down into her shoulder blade with a great crackling and blazing of nerves. It was not unusual for her daughter Alma to sit up the one or two nights that it could endure, unfailing through the wee hours in her chain of hot applications.

For a week, sometimes, these attacks heralded their comings with little jabs, like the pricks of an exploring needle. Then the under-eyes began to look their muddiest. They were darkening now and she put up two fingers with a little pressing movement to her temple.

"You're a great little woman," reiterated Mr. Latz, rather riveting even Mrs. Samstag's suspicion that here was no great stickler for variety of expression.

"I try to be," she said, his tone inviting out in her a mood of sweet forbearance.

"And a great sufferer, too," he said, noting the pressing fingers.

She colored under this delightful impeachment.

"I wouldn't wish one of my neuralgia spells to my worst enemy, Mr. Latz."

"If you were mine—I mean—if—the—say—was mine—I wouldn't stop until I had you to every specialist in Europe. I know a thing or two about those fellows over there. Some of them are wonders."

Mrs. Samstag looked off, her profile inclined to lift and fall as if by little pulleys of emotion.

"That's easier said than done, Mr. Latz, by a—widow who wants to do right by her grown daughter and living so—high since the war."

"I—I—" said Mr. Latz, leaping impulsively forward on the chair that was as tightly upholstered in effect as he in his modish suit, then clutching himself there as if he had caught the impulse on the fly, "I just wish I could help."

"Oh!" she said, and threw up a swift brown look from the lace making and then at it again.

He laughed, but from nervousness.

"My little mother was an ailer, too."

"That's me, Mr. Latz. Not sick—just ailing. I always say that it's ridiculous that a woman in such perfect health as I am should be such a sufferer."

"Same with her and her joints."

"Why, except for this old neuralgia, I can outdo Alma when it comes to dancing down in the grill with the young people of an evening, or shopping."

"More like sisters than any mother and daughter I ever saw."

"Mother and daughter, but which is which from the back, some of my friends put it," said Mrs. Samstag, not without a curve to her voice; then, hastily: "But the best child, Mr. Latz. The best that ever lived. A regular little mother to me in my spells."

"Nice girl, Alma."

"It snowed so the day of—my husband's funeral. Why, do you know that up to then I never had an attack of neuralgia in my life. Didn't even know what a headache was. That long drive. That windy hilltop with two men to keep me from jumping into the grave after him. Ask Alma. That's how I care when I care. But, of course, as the saying is, 'time heals.' But that's how I got my first attack. 'Intenseness' is what the doctors called it. I'm terribly intense."

"I—guess when a woman like you—cares like—you—cared, it's not much use hoping you would ever—care again. That's about the way of it, isn't it?"

If he had known it, there was something about his intensity of expression to inspire mirth. His eyebrows lifted to little Gothic arches of anxiety, a rash of tiny perspiration broke out over his blue shaved face, and as he sat on the edge of his chair it seemed that inevitably the tight sausagelike knees must push their way through mere fabric.

Ordinarily he presented the slightly bay-windowed, bay-rummed, spatted, and somewhat jowled well-being of the Wall Street bachelor who is a musical-comedy first-nighter, can dig the meat out of the lobster claw whole, takes his beefsteak rare and with two or three condiments, and wears his elk's tooth dangling from his waistcoat pocket and mounted on a band of platinum and tiny diamonds.

Mothers of debutantes were by no means unamiably disposed toward him, but the debutantes themselves slithered away like slim-flanked minnows.

It was rumored that one summer at the Royal Palisades Hotel in Atlantic City he had become engaged to a slim-flanked one from Akron, Ohio. But on the evening of the first day she had seen him in a bathing suit the rebellious young girl and a bitterly disappointed and remonstrating mother had departed on the Buck Eye for "points west."

There was almost something of the nudity of arm and leg he must have presented to eighteen's tender sensibilities in Mr. Latz's expression now as he sat well forward on the overstuffed chair, his overstuffed knees strained apart, his face nude of all pretense and creased with anxiety.

"That's about the way of it, isn't it?" he said again into the growing silence.

Suddenly Mrs. Samstag's fingers were rigid at their task of lace making, the scraping of the orchestral violin tearing the roaring noises in her ears into ribbons of alternate sound and vacuum, as if she were closing her ears and opening them, so roaringly the blood pounded.

"I—When a woman cares for—a man like—I did—Mr. Latz, she'll never be happy until—she cares again—like that. I always say, once an affectionate nature, always an affectionate nature."

"You mean," he said, leaning forward the imperceptible half inch that was left of chair—"you mean—me—?"

The smell of bay rum came out greenly then as the moisture sprang out on his scalp.

"I—I'm a home woman, Mr. Latz. You can put a fish in water, but you cannot make him swim. That's me and hotel life."

At this somewhat cryptic apothegm Mr. Latz's knee touched Mrs. Samstag's, so that he sprang back full of nerves at what he had not intended.

"Marry me, Carrie," he said, more abruptly than he might have, without the act of that knee to immediately justify.

She spread the lace out on her lap.

Ostensibly to the hotel lobby they were as casual as, "My mulligatawny soup was cold to-night," or, "Have you heard the new one that Al Jolson pulls at the Winter Garden?" But actually the roar was higher than ever in Mrs. Samstag's ears and he could feel the plethoric red rushing in flashes over his body.

"Marry me, Carrie," he said, as if to prove that his stiff lips could repeat their incredible feat.

With a woman's talent for them, her tears sprang.

"Mr. Latz—"

"Louis," he interpolated, widely eloquent of eyebrow and posture.

"You're proposing, Louis!" She explained rather than asked, and placed her hand to her heart so prettily that he wanted to crush it there with his kisses.

"God bless you for knowing it so easy, Carrie. A young girl would make it so hard. It's just what has kept me from asking you weeks ago, this getting it said. Carrie, will you?"

"I'm a widow, Mr. Latz—Louis—"

"Loo—"

"L—loo. With a grown daughter. Not one of those merry-widows you read about."

"That's me! A bachelor on top, but a home man underneath. Why, up to five years ago, Carrie, while the best little mother a man ever had was alive, I never had eyes for a woman or—"

"It's common talk what a grand son you were to her, Mr. La—Louis—"

"Loo."

"Loo."

"I don't want to seem to brag, Carrie, but you saw the coat that just walked out on Mrs. Gronauer? My little mother she was a humpback, Carrie, not a real one, but all stooped from the heavy years when she was helping my father to get his start. Well, anyway, that little stooped back was one of the reasons why I was so anxious to make it up to her. Y'understand?"

"Yes—Loo."

"But you saw that mink coat. Well, my little mother, three years before she died, was wearing one like that in sable. Real Russian. Set me back eighteen thousand, wholesale, and she never knew different than that it cost eighteen hundred. Proudest moment of my life when I helped my little old mother into her own automobile in that sable coat.

"I had some friends lived in the Grenoble Apartments when you did—the Adelbergs. They used to tell me how it hung right down to her heels and she never got into the auto that she didn't pick it up so as not to sit on it.

"That there coat is packed away in cold storage now, Carrie, waiting, without me exactly knowing why, I guess, for—the one little woman in the world besides her I would let so much as touch its hem."

Mrs. Samstag's lips parted, her teeth showing through like light.

"Oh," she said, "sable! That's my fur, Loo. I've never owned any, but ask Alma if I don't stop to look at it in every show window. Sable!"

"Carrie—would you—could you—I'm not what you would call a youngster in years, I guess, but forty-four isn't—"

"I'm—forty-one, Louis. A man like you could have younger."

"No. That's what I don't want. In my lonesomeness, after my mother's death, I thought once that maybe a young girl from the West, nice girl with her mother from Ohio—but I—funny thing, now I come to think about it—I never once mentioned my little mother's sable coat to her. I couldn't have satisfied a young girl like that, or her me, Carrie, any more than I could satisfy Alma. It was one of those mamma-made matches that we got into because we couldn't help it and out of it before it was too late. No, no, Carrie, what I want is a woman as near as possible to my own age."

"Loo, I—I couldn't start in with you even with the one little lie that gives every woman a right to be a liar. I'm forty-three, Louis—nearer to forty-four. You're not mad, Loo?"

"God love it! If that ain't a little woman for you! Mad? Why, just your doing that little thing with me raises your stock fifty per cent."

"I'm—that way."

"We're a lot alike, Carrie. For five years I've been living in this hotel because it's the best I can do under the circumstances. But at heart I'm a home man, Carrie, and unless I'm pretty much off my guess, you are, too—I mean a home woman. Right?"

"Me all over, Loo. Ask Alma if—"

"I've got the means, too, Carrie, to give a woman a home to be proud of."

"Just for fun, ask Alma, Loo, if one year since her father's death I haven't said, 'Alma, I wish I had the heart to go back housekeeping.'"

"I knew it!"

"But I ask you, Louis, what's been the incentive? Without a man in the house I wouldn't have the same interest. That first winter after my husband died I didn't even have the heart to take the summer covers off the furniture. Alma was a child then, too, so I kept asking myself, 'For what should I take an interest?' You can believe me or not, but half the time with just me to eat it, I wouldn't bother with more than a cold snack for supper, and everyone knew what a table we used to set. But with no one to come home evenings expecting a hot meal—"

"You poor little woman! I know how it is. Why, if I so much as used to telephone that I couldn't get home for supper, right away I knew the little mother would turn out the gas under what was cooking and not eat enough herself to keep a bird alive."

"Housekeeping is no life for a woman alone. On the other hand, Mr. Latz—Louis—Loo, on my income, and with a daughter growing up, and naturally anxious to give her the best, it hasn't been so easy. People think I'm a rich widow, and with her father's memory to consider and a young lady daughter, naturally I let them think it, but on my seventy-four hundred a year it has been hard to keep up appearances in a hotel like this. Not that I think you think I'm a rich widow, but just the same, that's me every time. Right out with the truth from the start."

"It shows you're a clever little manager to be able to do it."

"We lived big and spent big while my husband lived. He was as shrewd a jobber in knit underwear as the business ever saw, but—well, you know how it is. Pneumonia. I always say he wore himself out with conscientiousness."

"Maybe you don't believe it, Carrie, but it makes me happy what you just said about money. It means I can give you things you couldn't afford for yourself. I don't say this for publication, Carrie, but in Wall Street alone, outside of my brokerage business, I cleared eighty-six thousand last year. I can give you the best. You deserve it, Carrie. Will you say yes?"

"My daughter, Loo. She's only eighteen, but she's my shadow—I lean on her so."

"A sweet, dutiful girl like Alma would be the last to stand in her mother's light."

"But remember, Louis, you're marrying a little family."

"That don't scare me."

"She's my only. We're different natured. Alma's a Samstag through and through. Quiet, reserved. But she's my all, Louis. I love my baby too much to—to marry where she wouldn't be as welcome as the day itself. She's precious to me, Louis."

"Why, of course! You wouldn't be you if she wasn't. You think I would want you to feel different?"

"I mean—Louis—no matter where I go, more than with most children, she's part of me, Loo. I—Why, that child won't so much as go to spend the night with a girl friend away from me. Her quiet ways don't show it, but Alma has character! You wouldn't believe it, Louis, how she takes care of me."

"Why, Carrie, the first thing we pick out in our new home will be a room for her."

"Loo!"

"Not that she will want it long, the way I see that young rascal Friedlander sits up to her. A better young fellow and a better business head you couldn't pick for her. Didn't that youngster go out to Dayton the other day and land a contract for the surgical fittings for a big new clinic out there before the local firms even rubbed the sleep out of their eyes? I have it from good authority Friedlander Clinical Supply Company doubled their excess-profit tax last year."

A white flash of something that was almost fear seemed to strike Mrs. Samstag into a rigid pallor.

"No! No! I'm not like most mothers, Louis, for marrying their daughters off. I want her with me. If marrying her off is your idea, it's best you know it now in the beginning. I want my little girl with me—I have to have my little girl with me!"

He was so deeply moved that his eyes were embarrassingly moist.

"Why, Carrie, every time you open your mouth you only prove to me further what a grand little woman you are!"

"You'll like Alma, when you get to know her, Louis."

"Why, I do now! Always have said she's a sweet little thing."

"She is quiet and hard to get acquainted with at first, but that is reserve. She's not forward like most young girls nowadays. She's the kind of a child that would rather go upstairs evenings with a book or her sewing than sit down here in the lobby. That's where she is now."

"Give me that kind every time in preference to all these gay young chickens that know more they oughtn't to know about life before they start than my little mother did when she finished."

"But do you think that girl will go to bed before I come up? Not a bit of it. She's been my comforter and my salvation in my troubles. More like the mother, I sometimes tell her, and me the child. If you want me, Louis, it's got to be with her, too. I couldn't give up my baby—not my baby."

"Why, Carrie, have your baby to your heart's content! She's got to be a fine girl to have you for a mother, and now it will be my duty to please her as a father. Carrie, will you have me?"

"Oh, Louis—Loo!"

"Carrie, my dear!"

And so it was that Carrie Samstag and Louis Latz came into their betrothal.

* * * * *

None the less, it was with some misgivings and red lights burning high on her cheek bones that Mrs. Samstag at just after ten that evening turned the knob of the door that entered into her little sitting room.

The usual horrific hotel room of tight green-plush upholstery, ornamental portières on brass rings that grated, and the equidistant French engravings of lavish scrollwork and scroll frames.

But in this case a room redeemed by an upright piano with a green-silk-and-gold-lace-shaded floor lamp glowing by. Two gilt-framed photographs and a cluster of ivory knickknacks on the white mantel. A heap of handmade cushions. Art editions of the gift poets and some circulating-library novels. A fireside chair, privately owned and drawn up, ironically enough, beside the gilded radiator, its headrest worn from kindly service to Mrs. Samstag's neuralgic brow.

From the nest of cushions in the circle of lamp glow Alma sprang up at her mother's entrance. Sure enough, she had been reading, and her cheek was a little flushed and crumpled from where it had been resting in the palm of her hand.

"Mamma," she said, coming out of the circle of light and switching on the ceiling bulbs, "you stayed down so late."

There was a slow prettiness to Alma. It came upon you like a little dawn, palely at first and then pinkening to a pleasant consciousness that her small face was heart-shaped and clear as an almond, that the pupils of her gray eyes were deep and dark, like cisterns, and to young Leo Friedlander (rather apt the comparison, too) her mouth was exactly the shape of a small bow that had shot its quiverful of arrows into his heart.

And instead of her eighteen she looked sixteen, there was that kind of timid adolescence about her, and yet when she said, "Mamma, you stayed down so late," the bang of a little pistol shot was back somewhere in her voice.

"Why—Mr. Latz—and—I—sat and talked."

An almost imperceptible nerve was dancing against Mrs. Samstag's right temple. Alma could sense, rather than see, the ridge of pain.

"You're all right, mamma?"

"Yes," said Mrs. Samstag, and sat down on a divan, its naked greenness relieved by a thrown scarf of black velvet stenciled in gold.

"You shouldn't have remained down so long if your head is hurting," said her daughter, and quite casually took up her mother's beaded hand bag where it had fallen in her lap, but her fingers feeling lightly and furtively as if for the shape of its contents.

"Stop that," said Mrs. Samstag, jerking it back, a dull anger in her voice.

"Come to bed, mamma. If you're in for neuralgia, I'll fix the electric pad."

Suddenly Mrs. Samstag shot out her arm, rather slim-looking in the invariable long sleeve she affected, drawing Alma back toward her by the ribbon sash of her pretty chiffon frock.

"Alma, be good to mamma to-night! Sweetheart—be good to her."

The quick suspecting fear that had motivated Miss Samstag's groping along the beaded hand bag shot out again in her manner.

"Mamma—you haven't—?"

"No, no! Don't nag me. It's something else, Alma. Something mamma is very happy about."

"Mamma, you've broken your promise again."

"No! No! No! Alma, I've been a good mother to you, haven't I?"

"Yes, mamma, yes, but what—"

"Whatever else I've been hasn't been my fault—you've always blamed Heyman."

"Mamma, I don't understand."

"I've caused you worry, Alma—terrible worry. I know that. But everything is changed now. Mamma's going to turn over such a new leaf that everything is going to be happiness in this family."

"Dearest, if you knew how happy it makes me to hear you say that."

"Alma, look at me."

"Mamma, you—you frighten me."

"You like Louis Latz, don't you, Alma?"

"Why, yes, mamma. Very much."

"We can't all be young and handsome like Leo, can we?"

"You mean—?"

"I mean that finer and better men than Louis Latz aren't lying around loose. A man who treated his mother like a queen and who worked himself up from selling newspapers on the street to a millionaire."

"Mamma?"

"Yes, baby. He asked me to-night. Come to me, Alma; stay with me close. He asked me to-night."

"What?"

"You know. Haven't you seen it coming for weeks? I have."

"Seen what?"

"Don't make mamma come out and say it. For eight years I've been as grieving a widow to a man as a woman could be. But I'm human, Alma, and he—asked me to-night."

There was a curious pallor came over Miss Samstag's face, as if smeared there by a hand.

"Asked you what?"

"Alma, it don't mean I'm not true to your father as I was the day I buried him in that blizzard back there, but could you ask for a finer, steadier man than Louis Latz? It looks out of his face."

"Mamma, you—What—are you saying?"

"Alma?"

There lay a silence between them that took on the roar of a simoon and Miss Samstag jumped then from her mother's embrace, her little face stiff with the clench of her mouth.

"Mamma—you—No—no! Oh, mamma—oh—!"

A quick spout of hysteria seemed to half strangle Mrs. Samstag so that she slanted backward, holding her throat.

"I knew it. My own child against me. O God! Why was I born? My own child against me!"

"Mamma—you can't marry him. You can't marry—anybody."

"Why can't I marry anybody? Must I be afraid to tell my own child when a good man wants to marry me and give us both a good home? That's my thanks for making my child my first consideration—before I accepted him."

"Mamma, you didn't accept him. Darling, you wouldn't do a—thing like that!"

Miss Samstag's voice thickened up then quite frantically into a little scream that knotted in her throat, and she was suddenly so small and stricken that, with a gasp for fear she might crumple up where she stood, Mrs. Samstag leaned forward, catching her again by the sash.

"Alma!"

It was only for an instant, however. Suddenly Miss Samstag was her coolly firm little self, the bang of authority back in her voice.

"You can't marry Louis Latz."

"Can't I? Watch me."

"You can't do that to a nice, deserving fellow like him!"

"Do what?"

"That!"

Then Mrs. Samstag threw up both her hands to her face, rocking in an agony of self-abandon that was rather horrid to behold.

"O God! why don't you put me out of it all? My misery! I'm a leper to my own child!"

"Oh—mamma—!"

"Yes, a leper. Hold my misfortune against me. Let my neuralgia and Doctor Heyman's prescription to cure it ruin my life. Rob me of what happiness with a good man there is left in it for me. I don't want happiness. Don't expect it. I'm here just to suffer. My daughter will see to that. Oh, I know what is on your mind. You want to make me out something—terrible—because Doctor Heyman once taught me how to help myself a little when I'm nearly wild with neuralgia. Those were doctor's orders. I'll kill myself before I let you make me out something terrible. I never even knew what it was before the doctor gave his prescription. I'll kill—you hear?—kill myself."

She was hoarse. She was tear splotched so that her lips were slippery with them, and while the ague of her passion shook her, Alma, her own face swept white and her voice guttered with restraint, took her mother into the cradle of her arms and rocked and hushed her there.

"Mamma, mamma, what are you saying? I'm not blaming you, sweetheart. I blame him—Doctor Heyman—for prescribing it in the beginning. I know your fight. How brave it is. Even when I'm crossest with you, I realize. Alma's fighting with you dearest every inch of the way until—you're cured! And then—maybe—some day—anything you want! But not now. Mamma, you wouldn't marry Louis Latz now!"

"I would. He's my cure. A good home with a good man and money enough to travel and forget myself. Alma, mamma knows she's not an angel. Sometimes when she thinks what she's put her little girl through this last year she just wants to go out on the hilltop where she caught the neuralgia and lie down beside that grave out there and—"

"Mamma, don't talk like that!"

"But now's my chance, Alma, to get well. I've too much worry in this big hotel trying to keep up big expenses on little money and—"

"I know it, mamma. That's why I'm so in favor of finding ourselves a sweet, tiny little apartment with kitch—"

"No! Your father died with the world thinking him a rich man and they will never find out from me that he wasn't. I won't be the one to humiliate his memory—a man who enjoyed keeping up appearances the way he did. Oh, Alma, Alma, I'm going to get well now! I promise. So help me God if I ever give in to—it again."

"Mamma, please! For God's sake, you've said the same thing so often, only to break your promise."

"I've been weak, Alma; I don't deny it. But nobody who hasn't been tortured as I have can realize what it means to get relief just by—"

"Mamma, you're not playing fair this minute. That's the frightening part. It isn't only the neuralgia any more. It's just desire. That's what's so terrible to me, mamma. The way you have been taking it these last months. Just from—desire."

Mrs. Samstag buried her face, shuddering, down into her hands.

"O God! My own child against me!"

"No, mamma. Why, sweetheart, nobody knows better than I do how sweet and good you are when you are away from—it. We'll fight it together and win! I'm not afraid. It's been worse this last month because you've been nervous, dear. I understand now. You see, I—didn't dream of you and—Louis Latz. We'll forget—we'll take a little two-room apartment of our own, darling, and get your mind on housekeeping, and I'll take up stenography or social ser—"

"What good am I, anyway? No good. In my own way. In my child's way. A young man like Leo Friedlander crazy to propose and my child can't let him come to the point because she is afraid to leave her mother. Oh, I know—I know more than you think I do. Ruining your life! That's what I am, and mine, too!"

Tears now ran in hot cascades down Alma's cheeks.

"Why, mamma, as if I cared about anything—just so you—get well."

"I know. I know the way you tremble when he telephones, and color up when he—"

"Mamma, how can you?"

"I know what I've done. Ruined my baby's life, and now—"

"No!"

"Then help me, Alma. Louis wants me for his happiness. I want him for mine. Nothing will cure me like having a good man to live up to. The minute I find myself getting the craving for—it—don't you see, baby, fear that a good husband like Louis could find out such a thing about me would hold me back? See, Alma?"

"That's a wrong basis to start married life on—"

"I'm a woman who needs a man to baby her, Alma. That's the cure for me. Not to let me would be the same as to kill me. I've been a bad, weak woman, Alma, to be so afraid that maybe Leo Friedlander would steal you away from me. We'll make it a double wedding, baby!"

"Mamma! Mamma! I'll never leave you."

"All right, then, so you won't think your new father and me want to get rid of you, the first thing we'll pick out in our new home, he said it himself to-night, 'is Alma's room.'"

"I tell you it's wrong. It's wrong!"

"The rest with Leo can come later, after I've proved to you for a little while that I'm cured. Alma, don't cry! It's my cure. Just think, a good man! A beautiful home to take my mind off—worry. He said to-night he wants to spend a fortune, if necessary, to cure—my neuralgia."

"Oh, mamma! Mamma! if it were only—that!"

"Alma, if I promise on my—my life! I never felt the craving so little as I do—now."

"You've said that before—and before."

"But never with such a wonderful reason. It's the beginning of a new life. I know it. I'm cured!"

"Mamma, if I thought you meant it."

"I do. Alma, look at me. This very minute I've a real jumping case of neuralgia. But I wouldn't have anything for it except the electric pad. I feel fine. Strong. Alma, the bad times with me are over."

"Oh, mamma! Mamma, how I pray you're right."

"You'll thank God for the day that Louis Latz proposed to me. Why, I'd rather cut off my right hand than marry a man who could ever live to learn such a—thing about me."

"But it's not fair. We'll have to explain to him, dear, that we hope you're cured now, but—"

"If you do—if you do—I'll kill myself! I won't live to bear that! You don't want me cured. You want to get rid of me, to degrade me until I kill myself! If I was ever anything else than what I am now—to Louis Latz—anything but his ideal—Alma, you won't tell! Kill me, but don't tell—don't tell!"

"Why, you know I wouldn't, sweetheart, if it is so terrible to you. Never."

"Say it again."

"Never."

"As if it hasn't been terrible enough that you should have to know. But it's over, Alma. Your bad times with me are finished. I'm cured."

There were no words that Miss Samstag could force through the choke of her tears, so she sat cheek to her mother's cheek, the trembling she could no longer control racing through her like a chill.

"Oh—how—I hope so!"

"I know so."

"But wait a little while, mamma—just a year."

"No! No!"

"A few months."

"No, he wants it soon. The sooner the better at our age. Alma, mamma's cured! What happiness! Kiss me, darling. So help me God to keep my promises to you! Cured, Alma, cured."

And so in the end, with a smile on her lips that belied almost to herself the little run of fear through her heart, Alma's last kiss to her mother that night was the long one of felicitation.

And because love, even the talk of it, is so gamy on the lips of woman to woman, they lay in bed, heartbeat to heartbeat, the electric pad under her pillow warm to the hurt of Mrs. Samstag's brow, and talked, these two, deep into the stillness of the hotel night.

"I'm going to be the best wife to him, Alma. You see, the woman that marries Louis has to measure up to the grand ideas of her he got from his mother."

"You were a good wife once, mamma. You'll be it again."

"That's another reason, Alma; it means my—cure. Living up to the ideas of a good man."

"Mamma! Mamma! you can't backslide now—ever."

"My little baby, who's helped me through such bad times, it's your turn now, Alma, to be care free like other girls."

"I'll never leave you, mamma, even if—he—Latz—shouldn't want me."

"He will, darling, and does! Those were his words. 'A room for Alma.'"

"I'll never leave you!"

"You will! Much as Louis and I want you with us every minute, we won't stand in your way! That's another reason I'm so happy, Alma. I'm not alone any more now. Leo's so crazy over you, just waiting for the chance to—pop—"

"Shh—sh—h—h!"

"Don't tremble so, darling. Mamma knows. He told Mrs. Gronauer last night when she was joking him to buy a ten-dollar carnation for the Convalescent Home Bazaar, that he would only take one if it was white, because little white flowers reminded him of Alma Samstag."

"Oh, mamma!"

"Say, it is as plain as the nose on your face. He can't keep his eyes off you. He sells goods to Doctor Gronauer's clinic and he says the same thing about him. It makes me so happy, Alma, to think you won't have to hold him off any more."

"I'll never leave you. Never!"

Nevertheless, she was the first to drop off to sleep, pink there in the dark with the secret of her blushes.

Then for Mrs. Samstag the travail set in. Lying there with her raging head tossing this way and that on the heated pillow, she heard with cruel awareness the minutiae, all the faint but clarified noises that can make a night seem so long. The distant click of the elevator depositing a nighthawk. A plong of the bedspring. Somebody's cough. A train's shriek. The jerk of plumbing. A window being raised. That creak which lies hidden in every darkness, like a mysterious knee joint. By three o'clock she was a quivering victim to these petty concepts, and her pillow so explored that not a spot but was rumpled to the aching lay of he cheek.

Once Alma, as a rule supersensitive to her mother's slightest unrest, floated up for the moment out of her young sleep, but she was very drowsy and very tired, and dream tides were almost carrying her back as she said:

"Mamma, you all right?"

Simulating sleep, Mrs. Samstag lay tense until her daughter's breathing resumed its light cadence.

Then at four o'clock the kind of nervousness that Mrs. Samstag had learned to fear began to roll over her in waves, locking her throat and curling her toes and fingers and her tongue up dry against the roof of her mouth.

She must concentrate now—must steer her mind away from the craving!

Now then: West End Avenue. Louis liked the apartments there. Luxurious. Quiet. Residential. Circassian walnut or mahogany dining room? Alma should decide. A baby-grand piano. Later to be Alma's engagement gift from "mamma and—papa." No, "mamma and Louis." Better so.

How her neck and her shoulder blade and now her elbow were flaming with the pain. She cried a little, quite silently, and tried a poor, futile scheme for easing her head in the crotch of her elbow.

Now then: She must knit Louis some neckties. The silk-sweater stitch would do. Married in a traveling suit. One of those smart dark-blue twills like Mrs. Gronauer, junior's. Topcoat—sable. Louis' hair thinning. Tonic. O God! let me sleep! Please, God! The wheeze rising in her closed throat. That little threatening desire that must not shape itself! It darted with the hither and thither of a bee bumbling against a garden wall. No! No! Ugh! the vast chills of nervousness. The flaming, the craving chills of desire!

Just this last giving-in. This one. To be rested and fresh for him to-morrow. Then never again. The little beaded hand bag. O God! help me! That burning ache to rest and to uncurl of nervousness. All the thousand thousand little pores of her body, screaming each one to be placated. They hurt the entire surface of her. That great storm at sea in her head; the crackle of lightning down that arm—

"Let me see—Circassian walnut—baby grand—" The pores demanding, crying—shrieking—

It was then that Carrie Samstag, even in her lovely pink nightdress a crone with pain, and the cables out dreadfully in her neck, began by infinitesimal processes to swing herself gently to the side of the bed, unrelaxed inch by unrelaxed inch, softly and with the cunning born of travail.

It was actually a matter of fifteen minutes, that breathless swing toward the floor, the mattress rising after her with scarcely a whisper and her two bare feet landing patly into the pale-blue room slippers, there beside the bed.

Then her bag, the beaded one on the end of the divan. The slow, taut feeling for it and the floor that creaked twice, starting the sweat out over her.

It was finally after more tortuous saving of floor creaks and the interminable opening and closing of a door that Carrie Samstag, the beaded bag in her hand, found herself face to face with herself in the mirror of the bathroom medicine chest.

She was shuddering with one of the hot chills. The needle and little glass piston out of the hand bag and with a dry little insuck of breath, pinching up little areas of flesh from her arm, bent on a good firm perch, as it were.

There were undeniable pockmarks on Mrs. Samstag's right forearm. Invariably it sickened her to see them. Little graves. Oh! oh! little graves! For Alma. Herself. And now Louis. Just once. Just one more little grave—

And Alma, answering her somewhere down in her heartbeats: "No, mamma. No, mamma! No! No! No!"

But all the little pores gaping. Mouths! The pinching up of the skin. Here, this little clean and white area.

"No, mamma! No, mamma! No! No! No!"

"Just once, darling?" Oh—oh—little graves for Alma and Louis. No! No! No!

Somehow, some way, with all the little mouths still parched and gaping and the clean and quite white area unblemished, Mrs. Samstag found her back to bed. She was in a drench of sweat when she got there and the conflagration of neuralgia, curiously enough, was now roaring in her ears so that it seemed to her she could hear her pain.

Her daughter lay asleep, with her face to the wall, her flowing hair spread in a fan against the pillow and her body curled up cozily. The remaining hours of the night, in a kind of waking faint she could never find the words to describe, Mrs. Samstag, with that dreadful dew of her sweat constantly out over her, lay with her twisted lips to the faint perfume of that fan of Alma's flowing hair, her toes curling in and out. Out and in. Toward morning she slept. Actually, sweetly, and deeply, as if she could never have done with deep draughts of it.

She awoke to the brief patch of sunlight that smiled into their apartment for about eight minutes of each forenoon.

Alma was at the pretty chore of lifting the trays from a hamper of roses. She placed a shower of them on her mother's coverlet with a kiss, a deeper and dearer one, somehow, this morning.

There was a card, and Mrs. Samstag read it and laughed:

Good morning, Carrie.
Louis.

They seemed to her, poor dear, these roses, to be pink with the glory of the coming of the dawn.

* * * * *

On the spur of the moment and because the same precipitate decision that determined Louis Latz's successes in Wall Street determined him here, they were married the following Thursday in Lakewood, New Jersey, without even allowing Carrie time for the blue-twill traveling suit. She wore her brown-velvet, instead, looking quite modish, a sable wrap, gift of the groom, lending genuine magnificence.

Alma was there, of course, in a beautiful fox scarf, also gift of the groom, and locked in a pale kind of tensity that made her seem more than ever like a little white flower to Leo Friedlander, the sole other attendant, and who during the ceremony yearned at her with his gaze. But her eyes were squeezed tight against his, as if to forbid herself the consciousness that life seemed suddenly so richly sweet to her—oh, so richly sweet!

* * * * *

There was a time during the first months of the married life of Louis and Carrie Latz when it seemed to Alma, who in the sanctity of her lovely little ivory bedroom all appointed in rose enamel toilet trifles, could be prayerful with the peace of it, that the old Carrie, who could come pale and terrible out of her drugged nights, belonged to some grimacing and chimeric past. A dead past that had buried its dead and its hatchet.

There had been a month at a Hot Springs in the wintergreen heart of Virginia, and whatever Louis may have felt in his heart of his right to the privacy of these honeymoon days was carefully belied on his lips, and at Alma's depriving him now and then of his wife's company, packing her off to rest when he wanted a climb with her up a mountain slope or a drive over piny roads, he could still smile and pinch her cheek.

"You're stingy to me with my wife, Alma," he said to her upon one of these provocations. "I don't believe she's got a daughter at all, but a little policeman instead."

And Alma smiled back, out of the agony of her constant consciousness that she was insinuating her presence upon him, and resolutely, so that her fear for him should always subordinate her fear of him, she bit down her sensitiveness in proportion to the rising tide of his growing, but still politely held in check, bewilderment.

Once, these first weeks of their marriage, because she saw the dreaded signal of the muddy pools under her mother's eyes and the little quivering nerve beneath the temple, she shut him out of her presence for a day and a night, and when he came fuming up every few minutes from the hotel veranda, miserable and fretting, met him at the closed door of her mother's darkened room and was adamant.

"It won't hurt if I tiptoe in and sit with her," he pleaded.

"No, Louis. No one knows how to get her through these spells like I do. The least excitement will only prolong her pain."

He trotted off, then, down the hotel corridor, with a strut to his resentment that was bantam and just a little fighty.

That night as Alma lay beside her mother, holding off sleep and watching, Carrie rolled her eyes side-wise with the plea of a stricken dog in them.

"Alma," she whispered, "for God's sake! Just this once. To tide me over. One shot—darling. Alma, if you love me?"

Later there was a struggle between them that hardly bears relating. A lamp was overturned. But toward morning, when Carrie lay exhausted, but at rest in her daughter's arms, she kept muttering in her sleep:

"Thank you, baby. You saved me. Never leave me, Alma. Never—never—never. You saved me, Alma."

And then the miracle of those next months. The return to New York. The happily busy weeks of furnishing and the unlimited gratifications of the well-filled purse. The selection of the limousine with the special body that was fearfully and wonderfully made in mulberry upholstery with mother-of-pearl caparisons. The fourteen-room apartment on West End Avenue with four baths, drawing-room of pink-brocaded walls, and Carrie's Roman bathroom that was precisely as large as her old hotel sitting room, with two full-length wall mirrors, a dressing table canopied in white lace over white satin, and the marble bath itself, two steps down and with rubber curtains that swished after.

There were evenings when Carrie, who loved the tyranny of things with what must have been a survival within her of the bazaar instinct, would fall asleep almost directly after dinner, her head back against her husband's shoulder, roundly tired out after a day all cluttered up with matching the blue upholstery of their bedroom with taffeta bed hangings. Shopping for a strip of pantry linoleum that was just the desired slate color. Calculating with electricians over the plugs for floor lamps. Herself edging pantry shelves in cotton lace.

Latz liked her so, with her fragrantly coiffured head, scarcely gray, back against his shoulder, and with his newspapers, Wall Street journals and the comic weeklies which he liked to read, would sit an entire evening thus, moving only when his joints rebelled, his pipe smoke carefully directed away from her face.

Weeks and weeks of this, and already Louis Latz's trousers were a little out of crease, and Mrs. Latz, after eight o'clock and under cover of a very fluffy and very expensive negligée, would unhook her stays.

Sometimes friends came in for a game of small-stake poker, but after the second month they countermanded the standing order for Saturday night musical-comedy seats. So often they discovered it was pleasanter to remain at home. Indeed, during these days of household adjustment, as many as four evenings a week Mrs. Latz dozed there against her husband's shoulder, until about ten, when he kissed her awake to forage with him in the great white porcelain refrigerator and then to bed.

And Alma. Almost she tiptoed through these months. Not that her scorching awareness of what must have lain low in Louis' mind ever diminished. Sometimes, although still never by word, she could see the displeasure mount in his face.

If she entered in on a tête-à-tête, as she did once, when by chance she had sniffed the curative smell of spirits of camphor on the air of a room through which her mother had passed, and came to drag her off that night to share her own lace-covered-and-ivory bed.

Again, upon the occasion of an impulsively planned motor trip and week-end to Long Beach, her intrusion had been so obvious.

"Want to join us, Alma?"

"Oh—yes—thank you, Louis."

"But I thought you and Leo were—"

"No, no. I'd rather go with you and mamma, Louis."

Even her mother had smiled rather strainedly. Louis' invitation, politely uttered, had said so plainly, "Are we two never to be alone, your mother and I?"

Oh, there was no doubt that Louis Latz was in love and with all the delayed fervor of first youth.

There was something rather throat-catching about his treatment of her mother that made Alma want to cry.

He would never tire of marveling, not alone at the wonder of her, but at the wonder that she was his.

"No man has ever been as lucky in women as I have, Carrie," he told her once in Alma's hearing. "It seemed to me that after—my little mother there couldn't ever be another—and now you!"

At the business of sewing some beads on a lamp shade Carrie looked up, her eyes dewy.

"And I felt that way about one good husband," she said, "and now I see there could be two."

Alma tiptoed out.

The third month of this she was allowing Leo Friedlander his two evenings a week. Once to the theater in a modish little sedan car which Leo drove himself. One evening at home in the rose-and-mauve drawing-room. It delighted Louis and Carrie slyly to have in their friends for poker over the dining-room table these evenings, leaving the young people somewhat indirectly chaperoned until as late as midnight. Louis' attitude with Leo was one of winks, quirks, slaps on the back, and the curving voice of innuendo.

"Come on in, Leo; the water's fine!"

"Louis!" This from Alma, stung to crimson and not arch enough to feign that she did not understand.

"Loo, don't tease," said Carrie, smiling, but then closing her eyes as if to invoke help to want this thing to come to pass.

But Leo was frankly the lover, kept not without difficulty on the edge of his ardor. A city youth with gymnasium-bred shoulders, fine, pole-vaulter's length of limb, and a clean tan skin that bespoke cold drubbings with Turkish towels.

And despite herself, Alma, who was not without a young girl's feelings for nice detail, could thrill to this sartorial sveltness and to the patent-leather lay of his black hair which caught the light like a polished floor.

In the lingo of Louis Latz, he was "a rattling good business man, too." He shared with his father partnership in a manufacturing business—"Friedlander Clinical Supply Company"—which, since his advent from high school into the already enormously rich firm, had almost doubled its volume of business.

The kind of sweetness he found in Alma he could never articulate even to himself. In some ways she seemed hardly to have the pressure of vitality to match his, but, on the other hand, just that slower beat to her may have heightened his sense of prowess.

His greatest delight seemed to lie in her pallid loveliness. "White honeysuckle," he called her, and the names of all the beautiful white flowers he knew. And then one night, to the rattle of poker chips from the remote dining room, he jerked her to him without preamble, kissing her mouth down tightly against her teeth.

"My sweetheart! My little white carnation sweetheart! I won't be held off any longer. I'm going to carry you away for my little moonflower wife."

She sprang back prettier than he had ever seen her in the dishevelment from where his embrace had dragged at her hair.

"You mustn't," she cried, but there was enough of the conquering male in him to read easily into this a mere plating over her desire.

"You can't hold me at arm's length any longer. You've maddened me for months. I love you. You love me. You do. You do," and crushed her to him, but this time his pain and his surprise genuine as she sprang back, quivering.

"No, I tell you. No! No! No!" and sat down trembling.

"Why, Alma!" And he sat down, too, rather palely, at the remote end of the divan.

"You—I—mustn't!" she said, frantic to keep her lips from twisting, her little lacy fribble of a handkerchief a mere string from winding.

"Mustn't what?"

"Mustn't," was all she could repeat and not weep her words.

"Won't—I—do?"

"It's—mamma."

"What?"

"Her."

"Her what, my little white buttonhole carnation?"

"You see—I—She's all alone."

"You adorable, she's got a brand-new husky husband."

"No—you don't—understand."

Then, on a thunderclap of inspiration, hitting his knee:

"I have it. Mamma-baby! That's it. My girlie is a cry-baby, mamma-baby!" And made to slide along the divan toward her, but up flew her two small hands, like fans.

"No," she said, with the little bang back in her voice which steadied him again. "I mustn't! You see, we're so close. Sometimes it's more as if I were the mother and she my little girl."

"Alma, that's beautiful, but it's silly, too. But tell me first of all, mamma-baby, that you do care. Tell me that first, dearest, and then we can talk."

The kerchief was all screwed up now, so tightly that it could stiffly unwind of itself.

"She's not well, Leo. That terrible neuralgia—that's why she needs me so."

"Nonsense! She hasn't had a spell for weeks. That's Louis' great brag, that he's curing her. Oh, Alma, Alma, that's not a reason; that's an excuse!"

"Leo—you don't understand."

"I'm afraid I—don't," he said, looking at her with a sudden intensity that startled her with a quick suspicion of his suspicions, but then he smiled.

"Alma!" he said, "Alma!"

Misery made her dumb.

"Why, don't you know, dear, that your mother is better able to take care of herself than you are? She's bigger and stronger. You—you're a little white flower, that I want to wear on my heart."

"Leo—give me time. Let me think."

"A thousand thinks, Alma, but I love you. I love you and want so terribly for you to love me back."

"I—do."

"Then tell me with kisses."

Again she pressed him to arm's length.

"Please, Leo! Not yet. Let me think. Just one day. To-morrow."

"No, no! Now!"

"To-morrow."

"When?"

"Evening."

"No, morning."

"All right, Leo—to-morrow morning—"

"I'll sit up all night and count every second in every minute and every minute in every hour."

She put up her soft little fingers to his lips.

"Dear boy," she said.

And then they kissed, and after a little swoon to his nearness she struggled like a caught bird and a guilty one.

"Please go, Leo," she said. "Leave me alone—"

"Little mamma-baby sweetheart," he said. "I'll build you a nest right next to hers. Good night, little white flower. I'll be waiting, and remember, counting every second of every minute and every minute of every hour."

For a long time she remained where he had left her, forward on the pink divan, her head with a listening look to it, as if waiting an answer for the prayers that she sent up.

* * * * *

At two o'clock that morning, by what intuition she would never know, and with such leverage that she landed out of bed plump on her two feet, Alma, with all her faculties into trace like fire horses, sprang out of sleep.

It was a matter of twenty steps across the hall. In the white-tiled Roman bathroom, the muddy circles suddenly out and angry beneath her eyes, her mother was standing before one of the full-length mirrors—snickering.

There was a fresh little grave on the inside of her right forearm.

* * * * *

Sometimes in the weeks that followed a sense of the miracle of what was happening would clutch at Alma's throat like a fear.

Louis did not know.

That the old neuralgic recurrences were more frequent again, yes. Already plans for a summer trip abroad, on a curative mission bent, were taking shape. There was a famous nerve specialist, the one who had worked such wonders on his mother's cruelly rheumatic limbs, reassuringly foremost in his mind.

But except that there were not infrequent and sometimes twenty-four-hour sieges when he was denied the sight of his wife, he had learned, with a male's acquiescence to the frailties of the other sex, to submit, and, with no great understanding of pain, to condone.

And as if to atone for these more or less frequent lapses, there was something pathetic, even a little heartbreaking, in Carrie's zeal for his well-being. No duty too small. One night she wanted to unlace his shoes and even shine them—would have, in fact, except for his fierce catching of her into his arms and for some reason his tonsils aching as he kissed her.

Once after a "spell" she took out every garment from his wardrobe and, kissing them piece by piece, put them back again, and he found her so, and they cried together, he of happiness.

In his utter beatitude, even his resentment of Alma continued to grow but slowly. Once, when after forty-eight hours she forbade him rather fiercely an entrance into his wife's room, he shoved her aside almost rudely, but, at Carrie's little shriek of remonstrance from the darkened room, backed out shamefacedly, and apologized next day in the conciliatory language of a tiny wrist watch.

But a break came, as she knew and feared it must.

One evening during one of these attacks, when for two days Carrie had not appeared at the dinner table, Alma, entering when the meal was almost over, seated herself rather exhaustedly at her mother's place opposite her stepfather.

He had reached the stage when that little unconscious usurpation in itself could annoy him.

"How's your mother?" he asked, dourly for him.

"She's asleep."

"Funny. This is the third attack this month, and each time it lasts longer. Confound that neuralgia!"

"She's easier now."

He pushed back his plate.

"Then I'll go in and sit with her while she sleeps."

She, who was so fastidiously dainty of manner, half rose, spilling her soup.

"No," she said, "you mustn't! Not now!" And sat down again hurriedly, wanting not to appear perturbed.

A curious thing happened then to Louis. His lower lip came pursing out like a little shelf and a hitherto unsuspected look of pigginess fattened over his rather plump face.

"You quit butting into me and my wife's affairs, you, or get the hell out of here," he said, without raising his voice or his manner.

She placed her hand to the almost unbearable flutter of her heart.

"Louis! You mustn't talk like that to—me!"

"Don't make me say something I'll regret. You! Only take this tip, you! There's one of two things you better do. Quit trying to come between me and her or—get out."

"I—She's sick."

"Naw, she ain't. Not as sick as you make out. You're trying, God knows why, to keep us apart. I've watched you. I know your sneaking kind. Still water runs deep. You've never missed a chance since we're married to keep us apart. Shame!"

"I—She—"

"Now mark my word, if it wasn't to spare her I'd have invited you out long ago. Haven't you got any pride?"

"I have. I have," she almost moaned, and could have crumpled up there and swooned her humiliation.

"You're not a regular girl. You're a she-devil. That's what you are! Trying to come between your mother and me. Ain't you ashamed? What is it you want?"

"Louis—I don't—"

"First you turn down a fine fellow like Leo Friedlander, so he don't come to the house any more, and then you take out on us whatever is eating you, by trying to come between me and the finest woman that ever lived. Shame! Shame!"

"Louis!" she said, "Louis!" wringing her hands in a dry wash of agony, "can't you understand? She'd rather have me. It makes her nervous trying to pretend to you that she's not suffering when she is. That's all, Louis. You see, she's not ashamed to suffer before me. Why, Louis—that's all! Why should I want to come between you and her? Isn't she dearer to me than anything in the world, and haven't you been the best friend to me a girl could have? That's all—Louis."

He was placated and a little sorry and did not insist further upon going into the room.

"Funny," he said. "Funny," and, adjusting his spectacles, snapped open his newspaper for a lonely evening.

The one thing that perturbed Alma almost more than anything else, as the dreaded cravings grew, with each siege her mother becoming more brutish and more given to profanity, was where she obtained the soluble tablets.

The well-thumbed old doctor's prescription she had purloined even back in the hotel days, and embargo and legislation were daily making more and more furtive and prohibitive the traffic in drugs.

Once Alma, mistakenly, too, she thought later, had suspected a chauffeur of collusion with her mother and abruptly dismissed him, to Louis' rage.

"What's the idea?" he said, out of Carrie's hearing, of course. "Who's running this shebang, anyway?"

Again, after Alma had guarded her well for days, scarcely leaving her side, Carrie laughed sardonically up into her daughter's face, her eyes as glassy and without swimming fluid as a doll's.

"I get it! But wouldn't you like to know where? Yah!" And to Alma's horror slapped her quite roundly across the cheek so that for an hour the sting, the shape of the red print of fingers, lay on her face.

One night in what had become the horrible sanctity of that bedchamber— But let this sum it up. When Alma was nineteen years old a little colony of gray hairs was creeping in on each temple.

And then one day, after a long period of quiet, when Carrie had lavished her really great wealth of contrite love upon her daughter and husband, spending on Alma and loading her with gifts of jewelry and finery, somehow to express her grateful adoration of her, paying her husband the secret penance of twofold fidelity to his well-being and every whim, Alma, returning from a trip taken reluctantly and at her mother's bidding down to the basement trunk room, found her gone, a modish black-lace hat and the sable coat missing from the closet.

It was early afternoon, sunlit and pleasantly cold.

The first rush of panic and the impulse to dash after stayed, she forced herself down into a chair, striving with the utmost difficulty for coherence of procedure.

Where in the half hour of her absence had her mother gone? Matinée? Impossible! Walking? Hardly possible. Upon inquiry in the kitchen, neither of the maids had seen nor heard her depart. Motoring? With a hand that trembled in spite of itself Alma telephoned the garage. Car and chauffeur were there. Incredible as it seemed, Alma, upon more than one occasion, had lately been obliged to remind her mother that she was becoming careless of the old pointedly rosy hands. Manicurist? She telephoned the Bon Ton Beauty Parlors. No. Where? O God! Where? Which way to begin? That was what troubled her most. To start right so as not to lose a precious second.

Suddenly, and for no particular reason, Alma began a hurried search through her mother's dresser drawers of lovely personal appointments. Turning over whole mounds of fresh white gloves, delving into nests of sheer handkerchiefs and stacks of webby lingerie. Then for a while she stood quite helplessly, looking into the mirror, her hands closed about her throat.

"Please, God, where?"

A one-inch square of newspaper clipping, apparently gouged from the sheet with a hairpin, caught her eye from the top of one of the gold-backed hairbrushes. Dawningly, Alma read.

It described in brief detail the innovation of a newly equipped narcotic clinic on the Bowery below Canal Street, provided to medically administer to the pathological cravings of addicts.

Fifteen minutes later Alma emerged from the Subway at Canal Street, and, with three blocks toward her destination ahead, started to run.

At the end of the first block she saw her mother, in the sable coat and the black-lace hat, coming toward her.

Her first impulse was to run faster and yoo-hoo, but she thought better of it and, by biting her lips and digging her finger nails, was able to slow down to a casual walk.

Carrie's fur coat was flaring open and, because of the quality of her attire down there where the bilge waters of the city tide flow and eddy, stares followed her.

Once, to the stoppage of Alma's heart, she saw Carrie halt and say a brief word to a truckman as he crossed the sidewalk with a bill of lading. He hesitated, laughed, and went on.

Then she quickened her pace and went on, but as if with a sense of being followed, because constantly as she walked she jerked a step, to look back, and then again, over her shoulder.

A second time she stopped, this time to address a little nub of a woman without a hat and lugging one-sidedly a stack of men's basted waistcoats, evidently for home work in some tenement. She looked and muttered her un-understanding at whatever Carrie had to say, and shambled on.

Then Mrs. Latz spied her daughter, greeting her without surprise or any particular recognition.

"Thought you could fool me! Heh, Louis? I mean Alma."

"Mamma, it's Alma. It's all right. Don't you remember, we had this appointment? Come, dear."

"No, you don't! That's a man following. Shh-h-h-h, Louis! I was fooling. I went up to him in the clinic" (snicker) "and I said to him, 'Give you five dollars for a doctor's certificate.' That's all I said to him, or any of them. He's in a white carnation, Louis. You can find him by the—it on his coat lapel. He's coming! Quick—"

"Mamma, there's no one following. Wait, I'll call a taxi!"

"No, you don't! He tried to put me in a taxi, too. No, you don't!"

"Then the Subway, dearest. You'll sit quietly beside Alma in the Subway, won't you, Carrie? Alma's so tired."

Suddenly Carrie began to whimper.

"My baby! Don't let her see me. My baby! What am I good for? I've ruined her life. My precious sweetheart's life. I hit her once—Louis—in the mouth. It bled. God won't forgive me for that."

"Yes, He will, dear, if you come."

"It bled. Alma, tell him in the white carnation that mamma lost her doctor's certificate. That's all I said to him. Saw him in the clinic—new clinic—'give you five dollars for a doctor's certificate.' He had a white carnation—right lapel. Stingy. Quick!—following!"

"Sweetheart, please, there's no one coming."

"Don't tell! Oh, Alma darling—mamma's ruined your life! Her sweetheart baby's life."

"No, darling, you haven't. She loves you if you'll come home with her, dear, to bed, before Louis gets home and—"

"No. No. He mustn't see. Never this bad—was I, darling? Oh! Oh!"

"No, mamma—never—this bad. That's why we must hurry."

"Best man that ever lived. Best baby. Ruin. Ruin."

"Mamma, you—you're making Alma tremble so that she can scarcely walk if you drag her so. There's no one following, dear. I won't let anyone harm you. Please, sweetheart—a taxicab."

"No. I tell you he's following. He tried to put me into a taxicab. Followed me. Said he knew me."

"Then, mamma, listen. Do you hear? Alma wants you to listen. If you don't—she'll faint. People are looking. Now I want you to turn square around and look. No, look again. You see now, there's no one following. Now I want you to cross the street over there to the Subway. Just with Alma who loves you. There's nobody following. Just with Alma who loves you."

And then Carrie, whose lace hat was quite on the back of her head, relaxed enough so that through the enormous maze of the traffic of trucks and the heavier drags of the lower city, her daughter could wind their way.

"My baby! My poor Louis!" she kept saying. "The worst I've ever been. Oh—Alma—Louis—waiting—before we get there—Louis!"

It was in the tightest tangle of the crossing and apparently on this conjuring of her husband that Carrie jerked suddenly free of Alma's frailer hold.

"No—no—not home—now. Him. Alma!" And darted back against the breast of the down side of the traffic.

There was scarcely more than the quick rotation of her arm around with the spoke of a truck wheel, so quickly she went down.

It was almost a miracle, her kind of death, because out of all that jam of tonnage she carried only one bruise, a faint one, near the brow.

And the wonder was that Louis Latz, in his grief, was so proud.

"To think," he kept saying over and over again and unabashed at the way his face twisted—"to think they should have happened to me. Two such women in one lifetime as my little mother—and her. Fat little old Louis to have had those two. Why, just the memory of my Carrie—is almost enough. To think old me should have a memory like that—it is almost enough—isn't it, Alma?"

She kissed his hand.

That very same, that dreadful night, almost without her knowing it, her throat-tearing sobs broke loose, her face to the waistcoat of Leo Friedlander.

He held her close—very, very close. "Why, sweetheart," he said, "I could cut out my heart to help you! Why, sweetheart! Shh-h-h! Remember what Louis says. Just the beautiful memory—of—her—is—wonderful—"

"Just—the b-beautiful—memory—you'll always have it, too—of her—my mamma—won't you, Leo? Won't you?"

"Always," he said when the tight grip in his throat had eased enough.

"Say—it again—Leo."

"Always."

She could not know how dear she became to him then, because not ten minutes before, from the very lapel against which her cheek lay pressed, he had unpinned a white carnation.

BACK PAY

I set out to write a love story, and for the purpose sharpened a bright-pink pencil with a glass ruby frivolously at the eraser end.

Something sweet. Something dainty. A candied rose leaf after all the bitter war lozenges. A miss. A kiss. A golf stick. A motor car. Or, if need be, a bit of khaki, but without one single spot of blood or mud, and nicely pressed as to those fetching peg-top trouser effects where they wing out just below the skirt-coat. The oldest story in the world told newly. No wear out to it. Editors know. It's as staple as eggs or printed lawn or ipecac. The good old-fashioned love story with the above-mentioned miss, kiss, and, if need be for the sake of timeliness, the bit of khaki, pressed.

Just my luck that, with one of these modish tales at the tip of my pink pencil, Hester Bevins should come pounding and clamoring at the door of my mental reservation, quite drowning out the rather high, the lipsy, and, if I do say it myself, distinctly musical patter of Arline. That was to have been her name. Arline Kildane. Sweet, don't you think, and with just a bit of wild Irish rose in it?

But Hester Bevins would not let herself be gainsaid, sobbing a little, elbowing her way through the group of mental unborns, and leaving me to blow my pitch pipe for a minor key.

Not that Hester's isn't one of the oldest stories in the world, too. No matter how newly told, she is as old as sin, and sin is but a few weeks younger than love—and how often the two are interchangeable!

If it be a fact that the true lady is, in theory, either a virgin or a lawful wife, then Hester Bevins stands immediately convicted on two charges.

She was neither. The most that can be said for her is that she was honestly what she was.

"If the wages of sin is death," she said to a roadhouse party of roysterers one dawn, "then I've quite a bit of back pay coming to me." And joined in the shout that rose off the table.

I can sketch her in for you rather simply because of the hackneyed lines of her very, very old story. Whose pasts so quickly mold and disintegrate as those of women of Hester's stripe? Their yesterdays are entirely soluble in the easy waters of their to-days.

For the first seventeen years of her life she lived in what we might call Any American Town of, say, fifteen or twenty thousand inhabitants. Her particular one was in Ohio. Demopolis, I think. One of those change-engine-and-take-on-water stops with a stucco art-nouveau station, a roof drooping all round it, as if it needed to be shaved off like edges of a pie, and the name of the town writ in conch shells on a green slant of terrace. You know—the kind that first establishes a ten-o'clock curfew for its young, its dance halls and motion-picture theaters, and then sends in a hurry call for a social-service expert from one of the large Eastern cities to come and diagnose its malignant vice undergrowth.

Hester Bevins, of a mother who died bearing her and one of those disappearing fathers who can speed away after the accident without even stopping to pick up the child or leave a license number, was reared—no, grew up, is better—in the home of an aunt. A blond aunt with many gold teeth and many pink and blue wrappers.

Whatever Hester knew of the kind of home that fostered her, it left apparently no welt across her sensibilities. It was a rather poor house, an unpainted frame in a poor street, but there was never a lack of gayety or, for that matter, any pinching lack of funds. It was an actual fact that, at thirteen, cotton or lisle stockings brought out a little irritated rash on Hester's slim young legs, and she wore silk. Abominations, it is true, at three pair for a dollar, that sprang runs and would not hold a darn, but, just the same, they were silk. There was an air of easy *camaraderie* and easy money about that house. It was not unusual for her to come home from school at high noon and find a front-room group of one, two, three, or four guests, almost invariably men. Frequently these guests handed her out as much as half a dollar for candy money, and not another child in school reckoned in more than pennies.

Once a guest, for reasons of odd change, I suppose, handed her out thirteen cents. Outraged, at the meanness of the sum, and with an early and deep-dyed superstition of thirteen, she dashed the coins out of his hand and to the four corners of the room, escaping in the guffaw of laughter that went up.

Often her childish sleep in a small top room with slanting sides would be broken upon by loud ribaldry that lasted into dawn, but never by word, and certainly not by deed, was she to know from her aunt any of its sordid significance.

Literally, Hester Bevins was left to feather her own nest. There were no demands made upon her. Once, in the little atrocious front parlor of horsehair and chromo, one of the guests, the town baggage-master, to be exact, made to embrace her, receiving from the left rear a sounding smack across cheek and ear from the aunt.

"Cut that! Hester, go out and play! Whatever she's got to learn from life, she can't say she learned it in my house."

There were even two years of high school, and at sixteen, when she went, at her own volition, to clerk in Finley's two-story department store on High Street, she was still innocent, although she and Gerald Fishback were openly sweethearts.

Gerald was a Thor. Of course, you are not to take that literally; but if ever there was a carnification of the great god himself, then Gerald was in his image. A wide streak of the Scandinavian ran through his make-up, although he had been born in Middletown, and from there had come recently to the Finley Dry Goods Company as an accountant.

He was so the viking in his bigness that once, on a picnic, he had carried two girls, screaming their fun, across twenty feet of stream. Hester was one of them.

It was at this picnic, the Finley annual, that he asked Hester, then seventeen, to marry him. She was darkly, wildly pretty, as a rambler rose tugging at its stem is restlessly pretty, as a pointed little gazelle smelling up at the moon is whimsically pretty, as a runaway stream from off the flank of a river is naughtily pretty, and she wore a crisp percale shirt waist with a saucy bow at the collar, fifty-cent silk stockings, and already she had almond incarnadine nails with points to them.

They were in the very heart of Wallach's Grove, under a natural cathedral of trees, the noises of the revelers and the small explosions of soda-water and beer bottles almost remote enough for perfect quiet. He was stretched his full and splendid length at the picknickers' immemorial business of plucking and sucking grass blades, and she seated very trimly, her little blue-serge skirt crawling up ever so slightly to reveal the silken ankle, on a rock beside him.

"Tickle-tickle!" she cried, with some of that irrepressible animal spirit of hers, and leaning to brush his ear with a twig.

He caught at her hand.

"Hester," he said, "marry me."

She felt a foaming through her until her finger tips sang.

"Well, I like that!" was what she said, though, and flung up a pointed profile that was like that same gazelle's smelling the moon.

He was very darkly red, and rose to his knees to clasp her about the waist. She felt like relaxing back against his blondness and feeling her fingers plow through the great double wave of his hair. But she did not.

"You're too poor," she said.

He sat back without speaking for a long minute.

"Money isn't everything," he said, finally, and with something gone from his voice.

"I know," she said, looking off; "but it's a great deal if you happen to want it more than anything else in the world."

"Then, if that's how you feel about it, Hester, next to wanting you, I want it, too, more than anything else in the world."

"There's no future in bookkeeping."

"I know a fellow in Cincinnati who's a hundred-and-fifty-dollar man. Hester? Dear?"

"A week?"

"Why, of course not, dear—a month!"

"Faugh!" she said, still looking off.

He felt out for her hand, at the touch of her reddening up again.

"Hester," he said, "you're the most beautiful, the most exciting, the most maddening, the most—the most everything girl in the world! You're not going to have an easy time of it, Hester, with your—your environment and your dangerousness, if you don't settle down—quick, with some strong fellow to take care of you. A fellow who loves you. That's me, Hester. I want to make a little home for you and protect you. I can't promise you the money—right off, but I can promise you the bigger something from the very start, Hester. Dear?"

She would not let her hand relax to his.

"I hate this town," she said.

"There's Cincinnati. Maybe my friend could find an opening there."

"Faugh!"

"Cincinnati, dear, is a metropolis."

"No, no! You don't understand. I hate littleness. Even little metropolises. Cheapness. I hate little towns and little spenders and mercerized stockings and cotton lisle next to my skin, and machine-stitched nightgowns. Ugh! it scratches!"

"And I—I just love you in those starchy white shirt waists, Hester. You're beautiful."

"That's just the trouble. It satisfies you, but it suffocates me. I've got a pink-crêpe-de-Chine soul. Pink crêpe de Chine—you hear?"

He sat back on his heels.

"It—Is it true, then, Hester that—that you're making up with that salesman from New York?"

"Why," she said, coloring—"why, I've only met him twice walking up High Street, evenings!"

"But it *is* true, isn't it, Hester?"

"Say, who was answering your questions this time last year?"

"But it *is* true, isn't it, Hester? Isn't it?"

"Well, of all the nerve!"

But it was.

* * * * *

The rest tells glibly. The salesman, who wore blue-and-white-striped soft collars with a bar pin across the front, does not even enter the story. He was only a stepping-stone. From him the ascent or descent, or whatever you choose to call it, was quick and sheer.

Five years later Hester was the very private, the very exotic, manicured, coiffured, scented, svelted, and strictly *de-luxe* chattel of one Charles G. Wheeler, of New York City and Rosencranz, Long Island, vice-president of the Standard Tractor Company, a member of no clubs but of the Rosencranz church, three lodges, and several corporations.

You see, there is no obvious detail lacking. Yes, there was an apartment. "Flat" it becomes under their kind of tenancy, situated on the windiest bend of Riverside Drive and minutely true to type from the pale-blue and brocade vernis-Martin parlor of talking-machine, mechanical piano, and cellarette built to simulate a music cabinet, to the pink-brocaded bedroom with a *chaise-longue* piled high with a small mountain of lace pillowettes that were liberally interlarded with paper-bound novels, and a spacious, white-marble adjoining bathroom with a sunken tub, rubber-sheeted shower, white-enamel weighing scales, and overloaded medicine chest of cosmetic array in frosted bottles, sleeping-, headache-, sedative powders, *et al.* There were also a negro maid, two Pomeranian dogs, and last, but by no means least, a private telephone inclosed in a hall closet and lighted by an electric bulb that turned on automatically to the opening of the door.

There was nothing sinister about Wheeler. He was a rather fair exponent of that amazing genus known as "typical New-Yorker," a roll of money in his pocket, and a roll of fat at the back of his neck. He went in for light checked suits, wore a platinum-and-Oriental-pearl chain across his waistcoat, and slept at a Turkish bath once a week; was once named in a large corporation scandal, escaping indictment only after violent and expensive skirmishes; could be either savage or familiar with waiters; wore highly manicured nails, which he regarded frequently in public, white-silk socks only; and maintained, on a twenty-thousand-a-year scale in the decorous suburb of Rosencranz, a decorous wife and three children, and, like all men of his code, his ethics were strictly double decked. He would not permit his nineteen-year-old daughter Marion so much as a shopping tour to the city without the chaperonage of her mother or a friend, forbade in his wife, a comely enough woman with a white unmarcelled coiffure and upper arms a bit baggy with withering flesh, even the slightest of shirtwaist V's unless filled in with net, and kept up, at an expense of no less than fifteen thousand a year—thirty the war year that tractors jumped into the war-industry class—the very high-priced, -tempered, -handed, and -stepping Hester of wild-gazelle charm.

Not that Hester stepped much. There were a long underslung roadster and a great tan limousine with yellow-silk curtains at the call of her private telephone.

The Wheeler family used, not without complaint, a large open car of very early vintage, which in winter was shut in with flapping curtains with isinglass peepers, and leaked cold air badly.

On more than one occasion they passed on the road—these cars. The long tan limousine with the shock absorbers, foot warmers, two brown Pomeranian dogs, little case of enamel-top bottles, fresh flowers, and outside this little jewel-case interior, smartly exposed, so that the blast hit him from all sides, a chauffeur in uniform that harmonized nicely with the tans and yellows. And then the grotesque caravan of the Azoic motor age, with its flapping curtains and ununiformed youth in visored cap at the wheel.

There is undoubtedly an unsavory aspect to this story. For purpose of fiction, it is neither fragrant nor easily digested. But it is not so unsavory as the social scheme which made it possible for those two cars to pass thus on the road, and, at the same time, Charles G. Wheeler to remain the unchallenged member of the three lodges, the corporations, and the Rosencranz church, with a memorial window in his name on the left side as you enter, and again his name spelled out on a brass plate at the end of a front pew.

No one but God and Mrs. Wheeler knew what was in her heart. It is possible that she did not know what the world knew, but hardly. That she endured it is not admirable, but then there were the three children, and, besides, she lived in a world that let it go at that. And so she continued to hold up her head in her rather poor, mute way, rode beside her husband to funerals, weddings, and to the college Commencement of their son at Yale. Scrimped a little, cried a little, prayed a little in private, but outwardly lived the life of the smug in body and soul.

But the Wheelers' is another story, also a running social sore; but it was Hester, you remember, who came sobbing and clamoring to be told.

As Wheeler once said of her, she was a darn fine clothes horse. There was no pushed-up line of flesh across the middle of her back, as the corsets did it to Mrs. Wheeler. She was honed to the ounce. The white-enameled weighing scales, the sweet oils, the flexible fingers of her masseur, the dumb-bells, the cabinet, salt-water, needle-spray, and vapor baths saw to that. Her skin, unlike Marion Wheeler's, was unfreckled, and as heavily and tropically white as a magnolia leaf, and, of course, she reddened her lips, and the moonlike pallor came out more than ever.

As I said, she was frankly what she was. No man looked at her more than once without knowing it. To use an awkward metaphor, it was before her face like an overtone; it was an invisible caul. The wells of her eyes were muddy with it.

But withal, she commanded something of a manner, even from Wheeler. He had no key to the apartment. He never entered her room without knocking. There were certain of his friends she would not tolerate, from one or another aversion, to be party to their not infrequent carousals. Men did not always rise from their chairs when she entered a room, but she suffered few liberties from them. She was absolutely indomitable in her demands.

"Lord!" ventured Wheeler, upon occasion, across a Sunday-noon, lace-spread breakfast table, when she was slim and cool fingered in orchid-colored draperies, and his newest gift of a six-carat, pear-shaped diamond blazing away on her right hand. "Say, aren't these Yvette bills pretty steep?

"One midnight-blue-and-silver gown $485.00
One blue-and-silver head bandeau 50.00
One serge-and-satin trotteur gown 275.00
One ciel-blue tea gown 280.00

"Is that the cheapest you can drink tea? Whew!"

She put down her coffee cup, which she usually held with one little finger poised elegantly outward as if for flight.

"You've got a nerve!" she said, rising and pushing back her chair. "Over whose ticker are you getting quotations that I come cheap?"

He was immediately conciliatory, rising also to enfold her in an embrace that easily held her slightness.

"Go on," he said. "You could work me for the Woolworth Building in diamonds if you wanted it badly enough."

"Funny way of showing it! I may be a lot of things, Wheeler, but I'm not cheap. You're darn lucky that the war is on and I'm not asking for a French car."

He crushed his lips to hers.

"You devil!" he said.

There were frequent parties. Dancing at Broadway cabarets, all-night joy rides, punctuated with road-house stop-overs, and not infrequently, in groups of three or four couples, ten-day pilgrimages to showy American spas.

"Getting boiled out," they called it. It was part of Hester's scheme for keeping her sveltness.

Her friendships were necessarily rather confined to a definite circle—within her own apartment house, in fact. On the floor above, also in large, bright rooms of high rental, and so that they were exchanging visits frequently during the day, often *en déshabillé*, using the stairway that wound up round the elevator shaft, lived a certain Mrs. Kitty Drew, I believe she called herself. She was plump and blond, and so very scented that her aroma lay on a hallway for an hour after she had scurried through it. She was well known and chiefly distinguished by a large court-plaster crescent which she wore on her left shoulder blade. She enjoyed the bounty of a Wall Street broker who for one day had attained the conspicuousness of cornering the egg market.

There were two or three others within this group. A Mrs. Denison, half French, and a younger girl called Babe. But Mrs. Drew and Hester were intimates. They dwaddled daily in one or the other's apartment, usually lazy and lacy with negligée, lounging about on the mounds of lingerie pillows over chocolates, cigarettes, novels, Pomeranians, and always the headache powders, nerve sedatives, or smelling salts, a running line of: "Lord! I've a head!" "I need a good cry for the blues!" "Talk about a dark-brown taste!" or, "There was some kick to those cocktails last night," through their conversation.

KITTY: "Br-r-r! I'm as nervous as a cat to-day."

HESTER: "Naughty, naughty bad doggie to bite muvver's diamond ring."

KITTY: "Leave it to you to land a pear-shaped diamond on your hooks."

HESTER: "He fell for it, just like that!"

KITTY: "You could milk a billiard ball."

HESTER: "I don't see any 'quality of mercy' to spare around your flat."

There were the two years of high school, you see.

"Ed's going out to Geyser Springs next month for the cure. I told him he could not go without me unless over my dead body, he could not."

"Geyser Springs. That's thirty miles from my home town."

"Your home town? Nighty-night! I thought you was born on the corner of Forty-second Street and Broadway with a lobster claw in your mouth."

"Demopolis, Ohio."

"What is that—a skin disease?"

"My last relation in the world died out there two years ago. An aunt. Wouldn't mind some Geyser Springs myself if I could get some of this stiffness out of my joints."

"Come on! I dare you! May Denison and Chris will come in on it, and Babe can always find somebody. Make it three or four cars full and let's motor out. We all need a good boiling, anyways. Wheeler looks about ready for spontaneous combustion, and I got a twinge in my left little toe. You on?"

"I am, if he is."

"If he is!' He'd fall for life in an Igorrote village with a ring in his nose if you wanted it."

And truly enough, it did come about that on a height-of-the-season evening a highly cosmopolitan party of four couples trooped into the solid-marble foyer of the Geyser Springs Hotel, motor coated, goggled, veiled; a whole litter of pigskin and patent-leather bags, hampers, and hat boxes, two golf bags, two Pomeranians, a bull in spiked collar, furs, leather coats, monogrammed rugs, thermos bottles, air pillows, robes, and an *ensemble* of fourteen wardrobe trunks sent by express.

They took the "cure." Rode horseback, motored, played roulette at the casino for big stakes, and scorned the American plan of service for the smarter European idea, with a special *à la carte* menu for each meal. Extraordinary-looking mixed drinks, strictly against the mandates of the "cure," appeared at their table. Strange midnight goings-on were reported by the more conservative hotel guests, and the privacy of their circle was allowed full integrity by the little veranda groups of gouty ladies or middle-aged husbands with liver spots on their faces. The bath attendants reveled in the largest tips of the season. When Hester walked down the large dining room evenings, she was a signal for the craning of necks for the newest shock of her newest extreme toilette. The kinds of toilettes that shocked the women into envy and mental notes of how the underarm was cut, and the men into covert delight. Wheeler liked to sit back and put her through her paces like a high-strung filly.

"Make 'em sit up, girl! You got them all looking like dimes around here."

One night she descended to the dining room in a black evening gown so daringly lacking in back, and yet, withal, so slimly perfect an elegant thing, that an actual breathlessness hung over the hall, the clatter of dishes pausing.

There was a gold bird of paradise dipped down her hair over one shoulder, trailing its smoothness like fingers of lace. She defied with it as she walked.

"Take it from me," said Kitty, who felt fat in lavender that night, "she's going it one too strong."

Another evening she descended, always last, in a cloth of silver with a tiny, an absurd, an impeccably tight silver turban dipped down over one eye, and absolutely devoid of jewels except the pear-shaped diamond on her left forefinger.

They were a noisy, a spending, a cosmopolitan crowd of too-well-fed men and too-well-groomed women, ignored by the veranda groups of wives and mothers, openly dazzling and arousing a tremendous curiosity in the younger set, and quite obviously sought after by their own kind.

But Hester's world, too, is all run through with sharply defined social schisms.

"I wish that Irwin woman wouldn't always hang round our crowd," she said, one morning, as she and Kitty lay side by side in the cooling room after their baths, massages, manicures, and shampoos. "I don't want to be seen running with her."

"Did you see the square emerald she wore last night?"

"Fake. I know the clerk at the Synthetic Jewelry Company had it made up for her. She's cheap, I tell you. Promiscuous. Who ever heard of anybody standing back of her? She knocks around. She sells her old clothes to Tessie, my manicurist. I've got a line on her. She's cheap."

Kitty, who lay with her face under a white mud of cold cream and her little mouth merely a hole, turned on her elbow.

"We can't all be top-notchers, Hester," she said. "You're hard as nails."

"I guess I am, but you've got to be to play this game. The ones who aren't end up by stuffing the keyhole and turning on the gas. You've got to play it hard or not at all. If you've got the name, you might as well have the game."

"If I had it to do over again—well, there would be one more wife-and-mother role being played in this little old world, even if I had to play it on a South Dakota farm."

"'Whatever is worth doing is worth doing well,' I used to write in a copy book. Well, that's the way I feel about this. To me, anything is worth doing to escape the cotton stockings and lisle next to your skin. I admit I never sit down and *think*. You know, sit down and take stock of myself. What's the use thinking? Live! Yes," mused Hester, her arms in a wreath over her head, "I think I'd do it all over again. There's not been so many, at that. Three. The first was a salesman. He'd have married me, but I couldn't see it on six thousand a year. Nice fellow, too—an easy spender in a small way, but I couldn't see a future to ladies' neckwear. I hear he made good later in munitions. Al was a pretty good sort, too, but tight. How I hate tightness! I've been pretty lucky in the long run, I guess."

"Did I say 'hard as nails'?" said Kitty, grotesquely fitting a cigarette in the aperture of her mouth. "I apologize. Why, alongside of you a piece of flint is morning cereal. Haven't you ever had a love affair? I've been married twice—that's how chicken hearted I can be. Haven't you ever pumped a little faster just because a certain some one walked into the room?"

"Once."

"Once what?"

"I liked a fellow. Pretty much. A blond. Say, he was blond! I always think to myself, Kit, next to Gerald, you've got the bluest eyes under heaven. Only, his didn't have any dregs."

"Thanks, dearie."

"I sometimes wonder about Gerald. I ought to drive over while we're out here. Poor old Gerald Fishback!"

"Sweet name—'Fishback.' No wonder you went wrong, dearie."

"Oh, I'm not getting soft. I saw my bed and made it, nice and soft and comfy, and I'm lying on it without a whimper."

"You just bet your life you made it up nice and comfy! You've the right idea; I have to hand that to you. You command respect from them. Lord! Ed would as soon fire a teacup at me as not. But, with me, it pays. The last one he broke he made up to me with my opal-and-diamond beetle."

"Wouldn't wear an opal if it was set next to the Hope diamond."

"Superstitious, dearie?"

"Unlucky. Never knew it to fail."

"Not a superstition in my bones. I don't believe in walking under ladders or opening an umbrella in the house or sitting down with thirteen, but, Lordy! never saw the like with you! Thought you'd have the hysterics over that little old vanity mirror you broke that day out at the races."

"Br-r-r! I hated it."

"Lay easy, dearie. Nothing can touch you the way he's raking in the war contracts."

"Great—isn't it?"

"Play for a country home, dearie. I always say real estate and jewelry are something in the hand. Look ahead in this game, I always say."

"You just bet I've looked ahead."

"So have I, but not enough."

"Somehow, I never feel afraid. I could get a job to-morrow if I had to."

"Say, dearie, if it comes to that, with twenty pounds off me, there's not a chorus I couldn't land back in."

"I worked once, you know, in Lichtig's import shop."

"Fifth Avenue?"

"Yes. It was in between the salesman and Al. I sold two thousand five hundred dollars' worth of gowns the first week."

"Sure enough?"

"'Girl,' old man Lichtig said to me the day I quit—'girl,' he said, 'if ever you need this job again, comeback; it's waiting.'"

"Fine chance!"

"I've got the last twenty-five dollars I earned pinned away this minute in the pocket of the little dark-blue suit I wore to work. I paid for that suit with my first month's savings. A little dark-blue Norfolk, Lichtig let me have out of stock for twenty-seven fifty."

"Were they giving them away with a pound of tea?"

"Honest, Kitty, it was neat. Little white shirt waist, tan shoes, and one of those slick little five-dollar sailors, and every cent paid out of my salary. I could step into that outfit to-morrow, look the part, and land back that job or any other. I had a way with the trade, even back at Finley's."

"Here, hold my jewel bag, honey; I'm going to die of cold-cream suffocation if she don't soon come back and unsmear me."

"Opal beetle in it?"

"Yes, dearie; but it won't bite. It's muzzled with my diamond horseshoe."

"Nothing doing, Kit. Put it under your pillow."

"You better watch out. There's a thirteenth letter in the alphabet; you might accidentally use it some day. You're going to have a sweet time to-night, you are!"

"Why?"

"The boys have engaged De Butera to come up to the rooms."

"You mean the fortune teller over at the Stag Hotel?"

"She's not a fortune teller, you poor nervous wreck. She's the highest-priced spiritualist in the world. Moving tables—spooks—woof!"

"Faugh!" said Hester, rising from her couch and feeling with her little bare feet for the daintiest of pink-silk mules. "I could make tables move, too, at forty dollars an hour. Where's my attendant? I want an alcohol rub."

They did hold séance that night in a fine spirit of lark, huddled together in the *de-luxe* sitting room of one of their suites, and little half-hysterical shrieks and much promiscuous ribaldry under cover of darkness.

Madame de Butera was of a distinctly fat and earthy blondness, with a coarse-lace waist over pink, and short hands covered with turquoise rings of many shapes and blues.

Tables moved. A dead sister of Wheeler's spoke in thin, high voice. Why is it the dead are always so vocally thin and high?

A chair tilted itself on hind legs, eliciting squeals from the women. Babe spoke with a gentleman friend long since passed on, and Kitty with a deceased husband, and began to cry quite sobbily and took little sips of highball quite gulpily. May Denison, who was openly defiant, allowed herself to be hypnotized and lay rigid between two chairs, and Kitty went off into rampant hysteria until Wheeler finally placed a hundred-dollar bill over the closed eyes, and whether under it, or to the legerdemain of madam's manipulating hands, the tight eyes opened, May, amid riots of laughter, claiming for herself the hundred-dollar bill, and Kitty, quite resuscitated, jumping up for a table cancan, her yellow hair tumbling, and her china-blue eyes with the dregs in them inclined to water.

All but Hester. She sat off by herself in a peacock-colored gown that wrapped her body suavity as if the fabric were soaking wet, a band of smoky-blue about her forehead. Never intoxicated, a slight amount of alcohol had a tendency to make her morose.

"What's the matter, Cleo?" asked Wheeler, sitting down beside her and lifting her cool fingers one by one, and, by reason of some remote analogy that must have stirred within him, seeing in her a Nile queen. "What's the matter Cleo? Does the spook stuff get your goat?"

She turned on him eyes that were all troubled up, like waters suddenly wind-blown.

"God!" she said, her fingers, nails inward, closing about his arm. "Wheeler—can—can the—dead—speak?"

But fleeting as the hours themselves were the moods of them all, and the following morning there they were, the eight of them, light with laughter and caparisoned again as to hampers, veils, coats, dogs, off for a day's motoring through the springtime countryside.

"Where to?" shouted Wheeler, twisting from where he and Hester sat in the first of the cars to call to the two motor-loads behind.

"I thought Crystal Cave was the spot"—from May Denison in the last of the cars, winding her head in a scarlet veil.

"Crystal Cave it is, then."

"Is that through Demopolis?"

Followed a scanning of maps.

"Sure! Here it is! See! Granite City. Mitchell. Demopolis. Crystal Cave."

"Good Lord! Hester, you're not going to spend any time in that dump?"

"It's my home town," she replied, coldly. "The only relation I had is buried there. It's nothing out of your way to drop me on the court-house steps and pick me up as you drive back, I've been wanting to get there ever since we're down here. Wanting to stop by your home town you haven't seen in five years isn't unreasonable, is it?"

He admitted it wasn't, leaning to kiss her.

She turned to him a face soft, with one of the pouts he usually found irresistible.

"Honey," she said, "what do you think?"

"What?"

"Chris is buying May that chinchilla coat I showed you in Meyerbloom's window the day before we left."

"The deuce he is!" he said, letting go of her hand, but hers immediately covering his.

"She's wiring her sister in the 'Girlie Revue' to go in and buy it for her."

"Outrage—fifteen thousand dollars to cover a woman's back! Look at the beautiful scenery, honey! You're always prating about views. Look at those hills over there! Great—isn't it?"

"I wouldn't expect it, Wheeler, if it wasn't war year and you landing one big contract after another. I'd hate to see May show herself in that chinchilla coat when we could beat her to it by a wire. I could telegraph Meyerbloom himself. I bought the sable rug of him. I'd hate it, Wheeler, to see her and Chris beat us to it. So would you. What's fifteen thousand when one of your contracts alone runs into the hundred thousands? Honey?"

"Wire," he said, sourly, but not withdrawing his hand from hers.

* * * * *

They left her at the shady court-house steps in Demopolis, but with pleasantry and gibe.

"Give my love to the town pump."

"Rush the old oaken growler for me."

"So long!" she called, eager to be rid of them. "Pick me up at six sharp."

She walked slowly up High Street. Passers-by turned to stare, but otherwise she was unrecognized. There was a new five-and-ten-cent store, and Finley Brothers had added an ell. High Street was paved. She made a foray down into the little side street where she had spent those queerly remote first seventeen years of her life. How dim her aunt seemed! The little unpainted frame house was gone. There was a lumber yard on the site. Everything seemed to have shrunk. The street was narrower and dirtier than she recalled it.

She made one stop, at the house of Maggie Simms, a high-school chum. It was a frame house, too, and she remembered that the front door opened directly into the parlor and the side entrance was popularly used instead. But a strange sister-in-law opened the side door. Maggie was married and living in Cincinnati. Oh, fine—a master mechanic, and there were twins. She started back toward Finley's, thinking of Gerald, and halfway she changed her mind.

Maggie Simms married and living in Cincinnati. Twins! Heigh-ho! What a world! The visit was hardly a success. At half after five she was on her way back to the court-house steps. Stupid to have made it six!

And then, of course, and quite as you would have it, Gerald Fishback came along. She recognized his blondness long before he saw her. He was bigger and more tanned, and, as of old, carried his hat in his hand. She noticed that there were no creases down the front of his trousers, but the tweed was good and he gave off that intangible aroma of well-being.

She was surprised at the old thrill racing over her. Seeing him was like a stab of quick steel through the very pit of her being. She reached out, touching him, before he saw her.

"Gerald," she said, soft and teasingly.

It was actually as if he had been waiting for that touch, because before he could possibly have perceived her her name was on his lips.

"Hester!" he said, the blueness of his eyes flashing between blinks. "Not Hester?"

"Yes, Hester," she said, smiling up at him.

He grasped both her hands, stammering for words that wanted to come quicker than he could articulate.

"Hester!" he kept repeating. "Hester!"

"To think you knew me, Gerald!"

"Know you! I'd know you blindfolded. And how—I—You're beautiful, Hester! I think you've grown five years younger."

"You've got on, Gerald. You look it."

"Yes; I'm general manager now at Finley's."

"I'm so glad. Married?"

"Not while there's a Hester Bevins on earth."

She started at her own name.

"How do you know I'm not married?"

"I—I know—" he said, reddening up.

"Isn't there some place we can talk, Gerald? I've thirty minutes before my friends call for me."

"'Thirty minutes?'"

"Your rooms? Haven't you rooms or a room where we could go and sit down?"

"Why—why, no, Hester," he said, still red. "I'd rather you didn't go there. But here. Let's stop in at the St. James Hotel. There's a parlor."

To her surprise, she felt herself color up and was pleasantly conscious of her finger tips.

"You darling!" She smiled up at him.

They were seated presently in the unaired plush-and-cherry, Nottingham-and-Axminster parlor of a small-town hotel.

"Hester," he said, "you're like a vision come to earth."

"I'm a bad durl," she said, challenging his eyes for what he knew.

"You're a little saint walked down and leaving an empty pedestal in my dreams."

She placed her forefinger over his mouth.

"Sh-h!" she said. "I'm not a saint, Gerald; you know that."

"Yes," he said, with a great deal of boyishness in his defiance, "I do know it, Hester, but it is those who have been through the fire who can sometimes come out—new. It was your early environment."

"My aunt died on the town, Gerald, I heard. I could have saved her all that if I had only known. She was cheap, aunt was. Poor soul! She never looked ahead."

"It was your early environment, Hester. I've explained that often enough to them here. I'd bank on you, Hester—swear by you."

She patted him.

"I'm a pretty bad egg, Gerald. According to the standards of a town like this, I'm rotten, and they're about right. For five years, Gerald, I've—"

"The real *you* is ahead of—and not behind you, Hester."

"How wonderful," she said, "for you to feel that way, but—"

"Hester," he said, more and more the big boy, and his big blond head nearing hers, "I don't care about anything that's past; I only know that, for me, you are the—"

"Gerald," she said, "for God's sake!"

"I'm a two hundred-a-month man now, Hester. I want to build you the prettiest, the whitest little house in this town. Out in the Briarwood section. I'll make them kowtow to you, Hester; I—"

"Why," she said, slowly, and looking at him with a certain sadness, "you couldn't keep me in stockings, Gerald! The aigrettes on this hat cost more than one month of your salary."

"Good God!" he said.

"You're a dear, sweet boy just the same; but you remember what I told you about my crêpe-de-Chine soul."

"Just the same, I love you best in those crispy white shirt waists you used to wear and the little blue suits and sailor hats. You remember that day at Finleys' picnic, Hester, that day, dear, that you—you—"

"You dear boy!"

"But it—your mistake—it—it's all over. You work now, don't you, Hester?"

Somehow, looking into the blueness of his eyes and their entreaty for her affirmative, she did what you or I might have done. She half lied, regretting it while the words still smoked on her lips.

"Why, yes, Gerald; I've held a fine position in Lichtig Brothers, New York importers. Those places sometimes pay as high as seventy-five a week. But I don't make any bones, Gerald; I've not been an angel."

"The—the salesman, Hester?"—his lips quivering with a nausea for the question.

"I haven't seen him in four years," she answered, truthfully.

He laid his cheek on her hand.

"I knew you'd come through. It was your environment. I'll marry you to-morrow—to-day, Hester. I love you."

"You darling boy!" she said, her lips back tight against her teeth. "You darling, darling boy!"

"Please, Hester! We'll forget what has been."

"Let me go," she said, rising and pinning on her hat; "let me go—or—or I'll cry, and—and I don't want to cry."

"Hester," he called, rushing after her and wanting to fold her back into his arms, "let me prove my trust—my love—"

"Don't! Let me go! Let me go!"

At slightly after six the ultra cavalcade drew up at the court-house steps. She was greeted with the pleasantries and the gibes.

"Have a good time, sweetness?" asked Wheeler, arranging her rugs.

"Yes," she said, lying back and letting her lids droop; "but tired—very, very tired."

At the hotel, she stopped a moment to write a telegram before going up for the vapor bath, nap, and massage that were to precede dinner.

"Meyerbloom & Co., Furriers. Fifth Avenue, New York," it was addressed.

* * * * *

This is not a war story except that it has to do with profiteering, parlor patriots, and the return of Gerald Fishback.

While Hester was living this tale, and the chinchilla coat was enveloping her like an ineffably tender caress, three hundred thousand of her country's youths were at strangle hold across three thousand miles of sea, and on a notorious night when Hester walked, fully dressed in a green gown of iridescent fish scales, into the electric fountain of a seaside cabaret, and Wheeler had to carry her to her car wrapped in a sable rug, Gerald Fishback was lying with his face in Flanders mud, and his eye sockets blackly deep and full of shrapnel, and a lung-eating gas cloud rolling at him across the vast bombarded dawn.

* * * * *

Hester read of him one morning, sitting up in bed against a mound of lace-over-pink pillows, a masseuse at the pink soles of her feet. It was as if his name catapulted at her from a column she never troubled to read. She remained quite still, looking at the name for a full five minutes after it had pierced her full consciousness. Then, suddenly, she swung out of bed, tilting over the masseuse.

"Tessie," she said, evenly enough, "that will do. I have to hurry to Long Island to a base hospital. Go to that little telephone in the hall—will you?—and call my car."

But the visit was not so easy of execution. It required two days of red tape and official dispensation before she finally reached the seaside hospital that, by unpleasant coincidence, only a year before had been the resort hotel of more than one dancing orgy.

She thought she would faint when she saw him, jerking herself back with a straining of all her faculties. The blood seemed to drain away from her body, leaving her ready to sink, and only the watchful and threatening eye of a man nurse sustained her. He was sitting up in bed, and she would never have recognized in him anything of Gerald except for the shining Scandinavian quality of his hair. His eyes were not bandaged, but their sockets were dry and bare like the beds of old lakes long since drained. She had only seen the like in eyeless marble busts. There were unsuspected cheek bones, pitched now very high in his face, and his neck, rising above the army nightshirt, seemed cruelly long, possibly from thinness.

"Are you Hester?" whispered the man nurse.

She nodded, her tonsils squeezed together in an absolute knot.

"He called for you all through his delirium," he said, and went out. She stood at the bedside, trying to keep down the screams from her speech when it should come. But he was too quick for her.

"Hester," he said, feeling out.

And in their embrace, her agony melted to tears that choked and seared, beat and scalded her, and all the time it was he who held her with rigid arm, whispered to her, soothed down the sobs which tore through her like the rip of silk, seeming to split her being.

"Now—now! Why, Hester! Now—now—now! Sh-h! It will be over in a minute. You mustn't feel badly. Come now, is this the way to greet a fellow that's so darn glad to see you that nothing matters? Why I can see you, Hester. Plain as day in your little crispy waist. Now, now! You'll get used to it in a minute. Now—now—"

"I can't stand it, Gerald! I can't! Can't! Kill me, Gerald, but don't ask me to stand it!"

He stroked down the side of her, lingering at her cheek.

"Sh-h! Take your time, dear," he said, with the first furry note in his voice. "I know it's hard, but take your time. You'll get used to me. It's the shock, that's all. Sh-h!"

She covered his neck with kisses and scalding tears, her compassion for him racing through her in chills.

"I could tear out my eyes, Gerald, and give them to you. I could tear out my heart and give it to you. I'm bursting of pain. Gerald! Gerald!"

There was no sense of proportion left her. She could think only of what her own physical suffering might do in penance. She would willingly have opened the arteries of her heart and bled for him on the moment. Her compassion wanted to scream. She, who had never sacrificed anything, wanted suddenly to bleed at his feet, and prayed to do so on the agonized crest of the moment.

"There's a girl! Why, I'm going to get well, Hester, and do what thousands of others of the blinded are doing. Build up a new, a useful, and a busy life."

"It's not fair! It's not fair!"

"I'm ready now, except for this old left lung. It's burnt a bit, you see—gas."

"God! God!"

"It's pretty bad, I admit. But there's another way of looking at it. There's a glory in being chosen to bear your country's wounds."

"Your beautiful eyes! Your blue, beautiful eyes! O God, what does it all mean? Living! Dying! All the rotters, all the rat-eyed ones I know, scot-free and Gerald chosen. God! God! where are you?"

"He was never so close to me as now, Hester. And with you here, dear, He is closer than ever."

"I'll never leave you, Gerald," she said, crying down into his sleeve again. "Don't be afraid of the dark, dear; I'll never leave you."

"Nonsense!" he said, smoothing her hair that the hat had fallen away from.

"Never! Never! I wish I were a mat for you to walk on. I want to crawl on my hands and knees for you. I'll never leave you, Gerald—never!"

"My beautiful Hester!" he said, unsteadily, and then again, "Nonsense!"

But, almost on the moment, the man nurse returned and she was obliged to leave him, but not without throbbing promises of the to-morrow's return, and then there took place, downstairs in an anteroom, a long, a closeted, and very private interview with a surgeon and more red tape and filing of applications. She was so weak from crying that a nurse was called finally to help her through the corridors to her car.

Gerald's left lung was burned out and he had three, possibly four, weeks to live.

All the way home, in her tan limousine with the little yellow curtains, she sat quite upright, away from the upholstery, crying down her uncovered face, but a sudden, an exultant determination hardening in her mind.

* * * * *

That night a strange conversation took place in the Riverside Drive apartment. She sat on Wheeler's left knee, toying with his platinum chain, a strained, a rather terrible pallor out in her face, but the sobs well under her voice, and its modulation about normal. She had been talking for over two hours, silencing his every interruption until he had fallen quite still.

"And—and that's all, Wheeler," she ended up. "I've told you everything. We were never more than just—friends—Gerald and me. You must take my word for it, because I swear it before God."

"I take your word, Hester," he said, huskily.

"And there he lies, Wheeler, without—without any eyes in his head. Just as if they'd been burned out by irons. And he—he smiles when he talks. That's the awful part. Smiles like—well, I guess like the angel he—he almost is. You see, he says it's a glory to carry the wounds of his country. Just think! just think! that boy to feel that, the way he lies there!"

"Poor boy! Poor, poor boy!"

"Gerald's like that. So—so full of faith. And, Wheeler, he thinks he's going to get well and lead a useful life like they teach the blind to do. He reminds me of one of those Greek statues down at the Athens Café. You know— broken. That's it; he's a broken statue."

"Poor fellow! Poor fellow! Do something for him. Buy the finest fruit in the town for him. Send a case of wine. Two."

"I—I think I must be torn to pieces inside, Wheeler, the way I've cried."

"Poor little girl!"

"Wheeler?"

"Now, now," he said; "taking it so to heart won't do no good. It's rotten, I know, but worrying won't help. Got me right upset, too. Come, get it off your mind. Let's take a ride. Doll up; you look a bit peaked. Come now, and to-morrow we'll buy out the town for him."

"Wheeler?" she said. "Wheeler?"

"What?"

"Don't look, Wheeler. I've something else to ask of you—something queer."

"Now, now," he said, his voice hardening but trying to maintain a chiding note; "you know what you promised after the chinchilla—no more this year until—"

"No, no; for God's sake, not that! It's still about Gerald."

"Well?"

"Wheeler, he's only got four weeks to live. Five at the outside."

"Now, now, girl; we've been all over that."

"He loves me, Wheeler, Gerald does."

"Yes?" dryly.

"It would be like doing something decent—the only decent thing I've done in all my life, Wheeler, almost like doing something for the war, the way these women in the pretty white caps have done, and you know we—we haven't turned a finger for it except to—to gain—if I was to—to marry Gerald for those few weeks, Wheeler. I know it's a—rotten sacrifice, but I guess that's the only kind I'm capable of making."

He sat squat, with his knees spread.

"You crazy?" he said.

"It would mean, Wheeler, his dying happy. He doesn't know it's all up with him. He'd be made happy for the poor little rest of his life. He loves me. You see, Wheeler, I was his first—his only sweetheart. I'm on a pedestal, he says, in his dreams. I never told you—but that boy was willing to marry me, Wheeler, knowing—some—of the things I am. He's always carried round a dream of me, you see—no, you wouldn't see, but I've been—well, I guess sort of a medallion that won't tarnish in his heart. Wheeler, for the boy's few weeks he has left? Wheeler?"

"Well, I'll be hanged!"

"I'm not turning holy, Wheeler. I am what I am. But that boy lying out there—I can't bear it! It wouldn't make any difference with us—afterward. You know where you stand with me and for always, but it would mean the dying happy of a boy who fought for us. Let me marry that boy, Wheeler. Let his light go out in happiness. Wheeler? Please, Wheeler?" He would not meet her eyes. "Wheeler?"

"Go to it, Hester," he said, coughing about in his throat and rising to walk away. "Bring him here and give him the fat of the land. You can count on me to keep out of the way. Go to it," he repeated.

And so they were married, Hester holding his hand beside the hospital cot, the man nurse and doctor standing by, and the chaplain incanting the immemorial words. A bar of sunshine lay across the bed, and Gerald pronounced each "I will" in a lifted voice that carried to the four corners of the little room. She was allowed to stay that night past hospital hours, and they talked with the dusk flowing over them.

"Hester, Hester," he said, "I should have had the strength to hold out against your making this terrible sacrifice."

"It's the happiest hour of my life," she said, kissing him.

"I feel well enough to get up now, sweetheart."

"Gerald, don't force. You've weeks ahead before you are ready for that."

"But to-morrow, dear, home! In whose car are you calling for me to-morrow to take me *home*?"

"In a friend's, dearest."

"Won't I be crowding up our little apartment? Describe it again to me, dearest—our *home*."

"It's so little, Gerald. Three rooms and the littlest, babiest kitchen. When you're once up, I'll teach its every corner to you."

Tears seeped through the line where his lids had been, and it was almost more than she could bear.

"I'll make it up to you, though, Hester. I know I should have been strong enough to hold out against your marrying me, but I'll make it up. I've a great scheme; a sort of braille system of accountancy—"

"Please, Gerald—not now!"

"If only, Hester, I felt easier about the finances. Will your savings stand the strain? Your staying at home from your work this way—and then me—"

"Gerald dear, I've told you so often—I've saved more than we need."

"My girl!"

"My dear, my dear!" she said.

* * * * *

They moved him with hardly a jar in an army ambulance, and with the yellow limousine riding alongside to be of possible aid, and she had the bed stripped of its laces and cool with linen for him, and he sighed out when they placed him on it and would not let go her hand.

"What a feeling of space for so little a room!"

"It's the open windows, love."

He lay back tiredly.

"What sweet linen!"

"I shopped it for you."

"You, too—you're in linen, Hester?"

"A percale shirt waist. I shopped it for you, too."

"Give me your hand," he said, and pressed a string of close kisses into its palm.

The simplicity of the outrageous subterfuge amazed even her. She held hothouse grapes at two dollars a pound to his lips, and he ate them through a smile.

"Naughty, extravagant girl!" he said.

"I saw them on a fruit stand for thirty cents, and couldn't resist."

"Never mind; I'll make it up to you."

Later, he asked for braille books, turning his sightless face toward her as he studied, trying to concentrate through the pain in his lung.

"If only you wouldn't insist upon the books awhile yet, dear. The doctor says it's too soon."

"I feel so strong, Hester, with you near, and, besides, I must start the pot boiling."

She kissed down into the high nap of his hair, softly.

Evenings, she read to him newspaper accounts of his fellow-soldiers, and the day of the peace, for which he had paid so terribly, she rolled his bed, alone, with a great tugging and straining, to the open window, where the wind from the river could blow in against him and steamboat whistles shoot up like rockets.

She was so inexpressibly glad for the peace day. Somehow, it seemed easier and less blackly futile to give him up.

Of Wheeler for three running weeks she had not a glimpse, and then, one day, he sent up a hamper, not a box, but an actual trunk of roses, and she, in turn, sent them up the back way to Kitty's flat, not wanting even their fragrance released.

With Kitty there were little hurried confabs each day outside the apartment door in the hallway before the elevator shaft. A veil of awe seemed to wrap the Drew woman.

"I can't get it out of my head, Hester. It's like a fairy story, and, in another way, it's a scream—Wheeler standing for this."

"Sh-h, Kitty! His ears are so sensitive."

"Quit shushing me every time I open my mouth. Poor kid! Let me have a look at him. He wouldn't know."

"No! No!"

"God! if it wasn't so sad it would be a scream—Wheeler footing the bills!"

"Oh—you! Oh—oh—you!"

"All right, all right! Don't take the measles over it. I'm going. Here's some chicken broth I brought down. Ed sent it up to me from Sherry's."

But Hester poured it into the sink for some nameless reason, and brewed some fresh from a fowl she tipped the hallboy a dollar to go out and purchase.

She slept on a cot at the foot of his bed, so sensitive to his waking that almost before he came up to consciousness she was at his side. All day she wore the little white shirt waists, a starchy one fresh each morning, and at night scratchy little unlacy nightgowns with long sleeves and high yokes. He liked to run his hand along the crispness of the fabric.

"I love you in cool stuff, Hester. You're so cool yourself, I always think of you in the little white waist and blue skirt. You remember, dear—Finleys' annual?"

"I—I'm going to dress like that for you always, Gerald."

"I won't let you be going back to work for long, sweetheart. I've some plans up my sleeve, I have."

"Yes! Yes!"

But when the end did come, it was with as much of a shock as if she had not been for days expecting it. The doctor had just left, puncturing his arm and squirting into his poor tired system a panacea for the pain. But he would not react to it, fighting down the drowsiness.

"Hester," he said, suddenly, and a little weakly, "lean down, sweetheart, and kiss me—long—long—"

She did, and it was with the pressure of her lips to his that he died.

* * * * *

It was about a week after the funeral that Wheeler came back. She was on the *chaise-longue* that had been dragged out into the parlor, in the webbiest of white negligées, a little large-eyed, a little subdued, but sweetening the smile she turned toward him by a trick she had of lifting the brows.

"Hel-lo, Wheeler!" she said, raising her cheek to be kissed.

He trailed his lips, but did not seek her mouth, sitting down rather awkwardly and in the spread-kneed fashion he had.

"Well, girl—you all right?"

"You helped," she said.

"It gave me a jolt, too. I made over twenty-five thousand to the Red Cross on the strength of it."

"Thank you, Wheeler."

"Lord!" he said, rising and rubbing his hands together. "Give us a couple of fingers to drink, honey; I'm cotton-mouthed."

She reached languidly for a blue-enameled bell, lying back, with her arms dangling and her smile out. Then, as if realizing that the occasion must be lifted, turned her face to him.

"Old bummer!" she said, using one of her terms of endearment for him and two-thirds closing her eyes. Then did he stoop and kiss her roundly on the lips.

* * * * *

For the remainder of this tale, I could wish for a pen supernally dipped, or for a metaphysician's plating to my vernacular, or for the linguistic patois of that land off somewhere to the west of Life. Or maybe just a neurologist's chart of Hester's nerve history would help.

In any event, after an evening of musical comedy and of gelatinous dancing, Hester awoke at four o'clock the next morning out of an hour of sound sleep, leaping to her knees there in bed like a quick flame, her gesture shooting straight up toward the jointure of wall and ceiling.

"Gerald!" she called, her smoky black hair floating around her and her arms cutting through the room's blackness. "Gerald!" Suddenly the room was not black. It was light with the Scandinavian blondness of Gerald, the head of him nebulous there above the pink-satin canopy of her dressing table, and, more than that, the drained lakes of his sockets were deep with eyes. Yes, in all their amazing blueness, but queerly sharpened to steel points that went through Hester and through her as if bayonets were pushing into her breasts and her breathing.

"Gerald!" she shrieked, in one more cry that curdled the quiet, and sat up in bed, trembling and hugging herself, and breathing in until her lips were drawn shudderingly against her teeth like wind-sucked window shades.

"Gerald!" And then the picture did a sort of moving-picture fade-out, and black Lottie came running with her hair grotesquely greased and flattened to take out the kink, and gave her a drink of water with the addition of two drops from a bottle, and turned on the night light and went back to bed.

The next morning Hester carried about what she called "a head," and, since it was Wheeler's day at Rosencranz, remained in bed until three o'clock, Kitty curled at the foot of it the greater part of the forenoon.

"It was the rotten night did me up. Dreams! Ugh! dreams!"

"No wonder," diagnosed Kitty, sweetly. "Indigestion from having your cake and eating it."

At three she dressed and called for her car, driving down to the Ivy Funeral Rooms, a Gothic Thanatopsis, set, with one of those laughs up her sleeves in which the vertical city so loves to indulge, right in the heart of the town, between an automobile-accessory shop and a quick-lunch room. Gerald had been buried from there with simple flag-draped service in the Gothic chapel that was protected from the view and roar of the Elevated trains by suitably stained windows. There was a check in Hester's purse made out for an amount that corresponded to the statement she had received from the Ivy Funeral Rooms. And right here again, for the sake of your elucidation, I could wish at least for the neurologist's chart. At the very door to the establishment—with one foot across the threshold, in fact—she paused, her face tilted toward the corner where wall and ceiling met, and at whatever she saw there her eyes dilated widely and her left hand sprang to her bosom as if against the incision of quick steel. Then, without even entering, she rushed back to her car again, urging her chauffeur, at the risk of every speed regulation, homeward.

That was the beginning of purgatorial weeks that were soon to tell on Hester. They actually brought out a streak of gray through her hair, which Lottie promptly dyed and worked under into the lower part of her coiffure. For herself, Hester would have let it remain.

Wheeler was frankly perplexed. God knows it was bad enough to be called upon to endure streaks of unreasonableness at Rosencranz, but Hester wasn't there to show that side to him if she had it. To be pretty frank about it, she was well paid not to. Well paid! He'd done his part. More than nine out of ten would have done. Been made a jay of, if the truth was known. She was a Christmas-tree bauble and was expected to throw off holiday iridescence. There were limits!

"You're off your feed, girl. Go off by yourself and speed up."

"It's the nights, Gerald. Good God—I mean Wheeler! They kill me. I can't sleep. Can't you get a doctor who will give me stronger drops? He doesn't know my case. Nerves, he calls it. It's this head. If only I could get rid of this head!"

"You women and your nerves and your heads! Are you all alike? Get out and get some exercise. Keep down your gasoline bills and it will send your spirits up. There's such a thing as having it too good."

She tried to meet him in lighter vein after that, dressing her most bizarrely, and greeting him one night in a batik gown, a new process of dyeing that could be flamboyant and narrative in design. This one, a long, sinuous robe that enveloped her slimness like a flame, beginning down around the train in a sullen smoke and rushing up to her face in a burst of crimson.

He thought her so exquisitely rare that he was not above the poor, soggy device of drinking his dinner wine from the cup of her small crimson slipper, and she dangled on his knee like the dangerous little flame she none too subtly purported to be, and he spanked her quickly and softly across the wrists because she was too nervous to hold the match steadily enough for his cigar to take light, and then kissed away all the mock sting.

But the next morning, at the fateful four o'clock, and in spite of four sleeping-drops, Lottie on the cot at the foot of her bed, and the night light burning, she awoke on the crest of such a shriek that a stiletto might have slit the silence, the end of the sheet crammed up and into her mouth, and, ignoring all of Lottie's calming, sat up on her knees, her streaming eyes on the jointure of wall and ceiling, where the open, accusing ones of Gerald looked down at her. It was not that they were terrible eyes. They were full of the sweet blue, and clear as lakes. It was only that they knew. Those eyes *knew. They knew!* She tried the device there at four o'clock in the morning of tearing up the still unpaid check to the Ivy Funeral Rooms, and then she curled up in bed with her hand in the negro maid's and her face half buried in the pillow.

"Help me, Lottie!" she begged; "help me!"

"Law! Pore child! Gettin' the horrors every night thisaway! I've been through it before with other ladies, but I never saw a case of the sober horrors befoh. Looks like they's the worst of all. Go to sleep, child. I's holdin'."

You see, Lottie had looked in on life where you and I might not. A bird's-eye view may be very, very comprehensive, but a domestic's-eye view can sometimes be very, very close.

And then, one night, after Hester had beat her hands down into the mattress and implored Gerald to close his accusing eyes, she sat up in bed, waiting for the first streak of dawn to show itself, railing at the pain in her head.

"God! My head! Rub it, Lottie! My head! My eyes! The back of my neck!"

The next morning she did what you probably have been expecting she would do. She rose and dressed, sending Lottie to bed for a needed rest. Dressed herself in the little old blue-serge suit that had been hanging in the very back of a closet for four years, with a five-and two ten-dollar bills pinned into its pocket, and pressed the little blue sailor hat down on the smooth, winglike quality of her hair. She looked smaller, peculiarly, indescribably younger. She wrote Wheeler a note, dropping it down the mail-chute in the hall, and then came back, looking about rather aimlessly for something she might want to pack. There was nothing; so she went out quite bare and simply, with all her lovely jewels in the leather case on the upper shelf of the bedroom closet, as she had explained to Wheeler in the note.

That afternoon she presented herself to Lichtig. He was again as you would expect—round-bellied, and wore his cigar up obliquely from one corner of his mouth. He engaged her immediately at an increase of five dollars a week, and as she was leaving with the promise to report at eight-thirty the next morning he pinched her cheek, she pulling away angrily.

"None of that!"

"My mistake," he apologized.

She considered it promiscuous and cheap, and you know her aversion for cheapness.

Then she obtained, after a few forays in and out of brownstone houses in West Forty-fifth Street, one of those hall bedrooms so familiar to human-interest stories—the iron-bed, washstand, and slop-jar kind. There was a five-dollar advance required. That left her twenty dollars.

She shopped a bit then in an Eighth Avenue department store, and, with the day well on the wane, took a street car up to the Ivy Funeral Rooms. This time she entered, but the proprietor did not recognize her until she explained. As you know, she looked smaller and younger, and there was no tan car at the curb.

"I want to pay this off by the week," she said, handing him out the statement and a much-folded ten-dollar bill. He looked at her, surprised. "Yes," she said, her teeth biting off the word in a click.

"Certainly," he replied, handing her out a receipt for the ten.

"I will pay five dollars a week hereafter."

"That will stretch it out to twenty-eight weeks," he said, still doubtfully.

"I can't help it; I must."

"Certainly," he said, "that will be all right," but looked puzzled.

That night she slept in the hall bedroom in the Eighth Avenue, machine-stitched nightgown. She dropped off about midnight, praying not to awaken at four. But she did—with a slight start, sitting up in bed, her eyes where the wall and ceiling joined.

Gerald's face was there, and his blue eyes were open, but the steel points were gone. They were smiling eyes. They seemed to embrace her, to wash her in their fluid.

All her fear and the pain in her head were gone. She sat up, looking at him, the tears streaming down over her smile and her lips moving.

Then, sighing out like a child, she lay back on the pillow, turned over, and went to sleep.

* * * * *

And this is the story of Hester which so insisted to be told. I think she must have wanted you to know. And wanted Gerald to know that you know, and, in the end, I rather think she wanted God to know.

THE VERTICAL CITY

In the most vertical city in the world men have run up their dreams and their ambitions into slim skyscrapers that seem to exclaim at the audacity of the mere mortar that sustains them.

Minarets appear almost to tamper with the stars; towers to impale the moon. There is one fifty-six-story rococo castle, built from the five-and-ten-cent-store earnings of a merchant prince, that shoots upward with the beautiful rush of a Roman candle.

Any Manhattan sunset, against a sky that looks as if it might give to the poke of a finger, like a dainty woman's pink flesh, there marches a silhouetted caravan of tower, dome, and the astonished crests of office buildings.

All who would see the sky must gaze upward between these rockets of frenzied architecture, which are as beautiful as the terrific can ever be beautiful.

In the vertical city there are no horizons of infinitude to rest the eyes; rather little breakfast napkins of it showing between walls and up through areaways. Sometimes even a lunchcloth of five, six, or maybe sixty hundred stars or a bit of daylight-blue with a caul of sunshine across, hoisted there as if run up a flagpole.

It is well in the vertical city if the eyes and the heart have a lift to them, because, after all, these bits of cut-up infinitude, as many-shaped as cookies, even when seen from a tenement window and to the accompaniment of crick in the neck, are as full of mysterious alchemy over men's hearts as the desert sky or the sea sky. That is why, up through the wells of men's walls, one glimpse of sky can twist the soul with—oh, the bitter, the sweet ache that lies somewhere within the heart's own heart, curled up there like a little protozoa. That is, if the heart and the eyes have a lift to them. Marylin's had.

* * * * *

Marylin! How to convey to you the dance of her! The silver scheherazade of poplar leaves when the breeze is playful? No. She was far nimbler than a leaf tugging at its stem. A young faun on the brink of a pool, startled at himself? Yes, a little. Because Marylin's head always had a listening look to it, as if for a message that never quite came through to her. From where? Marylin didn't know and didn't know that she didn't know. Probably that accounted for a little pucker that could sometimes alight between her eyes. Scarcely a shadow, rather the shadow of a shadow. A lute, played in a western breeze? Once a note of music, not from a lute however, but played on a cheap harmonica, had caught Marylin's heart in a little ecstasy of palpitations, but that doesn't necessarily signify. Zephyr with Aurora playing? Laughter holding both his sides?

How Marylin, had she understood it, would have kicked the high hat off of such Miltonic phrasing. Ah, she was like—herself!

And yet, if there must be found a way to convey her to you more quickly, let it be one to which Marylin herself would have dipped a bow.

She was like nothing so much as unto a whole two dollars' worth of little five-cent toy balloons held captive in a sea breeze and tugging toward some ozonic beyond in which they had never swum, yet strained so naturally toward.

That was it! A whole two dollars' worth of tugging balloons. Red—blue—orange—green—silver, jerking in hollow-sided collisions, and one fat-faced pink one for ten cents, with a smile painted on one side and a tear on the other.

And what if I were to tell you that this phantom of a delight of a Marylin, whose hair was a sieve for sun and whose laughter a streamer of it, had had a father who had been shot to death on the underslinging of a freight car in one of the most notorious prison getaways ever recorded, and whose mother—but never mind right here; it doesn't matter to the opening of this story, because Marylin, with all her tantalizing capacity for paradox, while every inch a part of it all, was not at all a part of it.

For five years, she who had known from infancy the furtive Bradstreet of some of the vertical city's most notorious aliases and gang names, and who knew, almost by baptism of fire, that there were short cuts to an easier and weightier wage envelope, had made buttonholes from eight until five on the blue-denim pleat before it was stitched down the front of men's blue-denim shirts.

At sweet sixteen she, whose mother had borne her out of wed—well, anyway, at sweet sixteen, like the maiden in the saying, she had never been kissed, nor at seventeen, but at eighteen—

It was this way. Steve Turner—"Getaway," as the quick lingo of the street had him—liked her. Too well. I firmly believe, though, that if in the lurid heat lightning of so stormy a career as Getaway's the beauty of peace and the peace of beauty ever found moment, Marylin nestled in that brief breathing space somewhere deep down within the noisy cabaret of Getaway's being. His eyes, which had never done anything of the sort except under stimulus of the horseradish which he ate in quantities off quick-lunch counters, could smart to tears at the thought of her. And over the emotions which she stirred in him, and which he could not translate, he became facetious—idiotically so.

Slim and supine as the bamboo cane he invariably affected, he would wait for her, sometimes all of the six work-a-evenings of the week, until she came down out of the grim iron door of the shirt factory where she worked, his one hip flung out, bamboo cane bent almost double, and, in his further zeal to attitudinize, one finger screwing up furiously at a vacant upper lip. That was a favorite comedy mannerism, screwing at where a mustache might have been.

"Getaway!" she would invariably admonish, with her reproach all in the inflection and with the bluest blue in her eyes he had ever seen outside of a bisque doll's.

The peculiar joy, then, of linking her sweetly resisting arm into his; of folding over each little finger, so! until there were ten tendrils at the crotch of his elbow and his heart. Of tilting his straw "katy" forward, with his importance of this possession, so that the back of his head came out in a bulge and his hip, and then of walking off with her, so! Ah yes, so!

MARYLIN *(who had the mysterious little jerk in her laugh of a very young child)*: "Getaway, you're the biggest case!"

GETAWAY *(wild to amuse her further)*: "Hocus pocus, Salamagundi! I smell the blood of an ice-cream sundae!"

MARYLIN *(hands to her hips and her laughter full of the jerks)*: "Getaway, stop your monkeyshines. The cop has his eye on you!"

GETAWAY *(sobered)*: "C'm on!"

Therein lay some of the wonder of her freshet laughter. Because to Marylin a police officer was not merely a uniformed mentor of the law, designed chiefly to hold up traffic for her passing, and with his night stick strike security into her heart as she hurried home of short, wintry evenings. A little procession of him and his equally dread brother, the plain-clothes man, had significantly patrolled the days of her childhood.

Once her mother, who had come home from a shopping expedition with the inside pocket of her voluminous cape full of a harvest of the sheerest of baby things to match Marylin's blond loveliness—batiste—a whole bolt of Brussels lace—had bitten the thumb of a policeman until it hung, because he had surprised her horribly by stepping in through the fire escape as she was unwinding the Brussels lace.

Another time, from her mother's trembling knee, she had seen her father in a crowded courtroom standing between two uniforms, four fingers peeping over each of his shoulders!

A uniform had shot her father from the underpinnings of the freight car. Her mother had died with the phantom of one marching across her delirium. Even opposite the long, narrow, and exceedingly respectable rooming house in which she now dwelt a uniform had stood for several days lately, contemplatively.

There was a menacing flicker of them almost across her eyeballs, so close they lay to her experience, and yet how she could laugh when Getaway made a feint toward the one on her beat, straightening up into exaggerated decorum as the eye of the law, noting his approach, focused.

"Getaway," said Marylin, hop-skipping to keep up with him now, "why has old Deady got his eye on you nowadays?"

Here Getaway flung his most Yankee-Doodle-Dandy manner, collapsing inward at his extremely thin waistline, arms akimbo, his step designed to be a mincing one, and his voice as soprano as it could be.

"You don't know the half of it, dearie. I've been slapping granny's wrist, just like that. Ts-s-st!"

But somehow the laughter had run out of Marylin's voice. "Getaway," she said, stopping on the sidewalk, so that when he answered his face must be almost level with hers—"you're up to something again."

"I'm up to snuff," he said, and gyrated so that the bamboo cane looped a circle.

She almost cried as she looked at him, so swift was her change of mood, her lips trembling with the quiver of flesh that has been bruised.

"Oh, Getaway!" she said, "get away." And pushed him aside that she might walk on. He did not know, nor did she, for that matter, the rustling that was all of a sudden through her voice, but it was almost one of those moments when she could make his eyes smart.

But what he said was, "For the luvagod, whose dead?"

"Me, in here," she said, very quickly, and placed her hand to her flimsy blouse where her heart beat under it.

"Whadda you mean, dead?"

"Just dead, sometimes—as if something inside of me that can't get out had—had just curled up and croaked."

The walk from the shirt factory where Marylin worked, to the long, lean house in the long, lean street where she roomed, smelled of unfastidious bedclothes airing on window sills; of garbage cans that repulsed even high-legged cats; of petty tradesmen who, mysteriously enough, with aërial clotheslines flapping their perpetually washings, worked and sweated and even slept in the same sour garments. Facing her there on these sidewalks of slops, and the unprivacy of stoops swarming with enormous young mothers and puny old children, Getaway, with a certain fox pointiness out in his face, squeezed her arm until she could feel the bite of his elaborately manicured finger nails.

"Marry me, Marylin," he said, "and you'll wear diamonds."

In spite of herself, his bay-rummed nearness was not unpleasant to her. "Cut it out—here, Getaway," she said through a blush.

He hooked her very close to him by the elbow, and together they crossed through the crash of a street bifurcated by elevated tracks.

"You hear, Marylin," he shouted above the din. "Marry me and you'll wear diamonds."

"Getaway, you're up to something again!"

"Whadda you mean?"

"Diamonds on your twenty a week! It can't be done."

His gaze lit up with the pointiness. "I tell you, Marylin, I can promise you headlights!"

"How?"

"Never you bother your little head how; O.K., though."

"*How*, Getaway?"

"Oh—clean—if that's what's worrying you. Clean-cut."

"It *is* worrying me."

"Saw one on a little Jane yesterday out to Belmont race track. A fist-load for a little trick like her. And sparkle! Say, every time that little Jane daubed some whitewash on her little nosie she gave that grand stand the squints. That's what I'm going to do. Sparkle you up! With a diamond engagement ring. Oh boy! How's that? A diamond engagement ring!"

"Oh, Getaway!" she said, with her hand on the flutter of her throat and closing her eyes as if to imprison the vision against her lids. "A pure white one with lots of fire dancing around it." And little Marylin, who didn't want to want it, actually kissed the bare dot on her left ring finger where she could feel the burn of it, and there in the crowded street, where he knew he was surest of his privacy with her, he stole a kiss off that selfsame finger, too.

"I'll make their eyes hang out on their cheeks like grapes when they see you coming along, Marylin."

"I love them because they're so clear—and clean! Mountain water that's been filtered through pebbles."

"Pebbles is right! I'm going to dike you out in one as big as a pebble. And poils! Sa-y, they're what cost the spondulicks. A guy showed me a string of little ones no bigger than pimples. Know what? That little string could knock the three spots out of a thousand-dollar bond—I mean bill!"

It was then that something flashed out of Marylin's face. A shade might have been lowered; a candle blown out.

"Getaway," she said, with a quick little dig of fingers into his forearm, "you're up to something!"

"Snuff, I said."

"What did you mean by that word, 'bond'?"

"Who built a high fence around the word 'bond'?"

"Bonds! All that stuff in the newspapers about those messengers disappearing out of Wall Street with—bonds! Getaway, are you mixed up in that? Getaway!"

"Well, well! I like that! I had you doped out for fair and warmer to-day. The weather prophet didn't predict no brainstorm."

"That's not answering."

"Well, whadda you know! Miss Sherlock Holmes finds a corkscrew in the wine cellar and is sore because it's crooked!"

"Getaway—answer."

"Whadda you want me to answer, Fairylin? That I'm the master mind behind the—"

"It worries me so! You up in Monkey's room so much lately. You think I don't know it? I do! All the comings and goings up there. Muggs Towers sneaking up to Monkey's room in that messenger boy's suit he keeps wearing all the time now. He's no more messenger boy than I am. Getaway, tell me, you and Muggs up in Monkey's room so often? Footsteps up there! Yours!"

"Gawalmighty! Now it's my footsteps!"

"I know them! Up in Monkey's room, right over mine. I know how you sneak up there evenings after you leave me. It don't look nice your going into the same house where I live, Getaway, even if it isn't to see me. It don't look right from the outside!"

"Nobody can ever say I wanted to harm a hair of your little head. I even look the other way when I pass your door. That's the kind of a modest violet I am."

"It's not that, but the looks. That's the reason, I'll bet, if the truth's known, why Monkey squirmed himself into that room over mine—to hide your comings and goings as if they was to see me."

"Nothing of the kind!"

"Everything—up there—worries me so! Monkey's room right over mine. My ceiling so full of soft footsteps that frighten me. I know your footsteps, Getaway, just as well as anything. The ball-of-your-foot—squeak! The-ball-of-your-foot—squeak!"

"Well, that's a good one! The-ball-of-me-foot—squeak!"

"Everybody tiptoeing! Muggs! Somebody's stocking feet! Monkey's. Steps that aren't honest. All on my ceiling. Monkey never ought to have rented a room in a respectable house like Mrs. Granady's. Nobody but genteel young fellows holding down genteel jobs ever had that room before. Monkey passing himself off as Mr. James Pollard, or whatever it is he calls himself, just for the cover of a respectable house—or of me, for all I know. You could have knocked me down with a feather the first time I met him in the hall. If I did right I'd squeal."

"You would, like hell."

"Of course I wouldn't, but with Mrs. Granady trying to run a respectable house, only the right kind of young fellows and girls rooming there, it's not fair. Monkey getting his nose into a house like that and hatching God knows what! Getaway, what do you keep doing up in that room—all hours—you and all the pussyfooters?"

"That's the thanks a fellow gets for letting a straight word like 'marry' slip between his teeth; that's the thanks a fellow gets for honest-to-God intentions of trying to get his girl out of a shirt factory and dike her out in—"

"But, Getaway, if I was only sure it's all straight!"

"Well, if that's all you think of me—"

"All your big-gun talk about the ring. Of course I—I'd like it. How could a girl help liking it? But only if it's on the level. Getaway—you see, I hate to act suspicious all the time, but all your new silk shirts and now the new checked suit and all. It don't match up with your twenty-dollar job in the Wall Street haberdashery."

Then Getaway threw out one of his feints of mock surprise. "Didn't I tell you, Fairylin? Well, whadda you know about that? I didn't tell her, and me thinking I did."

"What, Getaway, what?"

"Why, I'm not working there any more. Why, Gawalmighty couldn't have pleased that old screwdriver. He was so tight the dimes in his pocket used to mildew from laying. He got sore as a pup at me one day just because I—"

"Getaway, you never told me you lost that job that I got for you out of the newspaper!"

"I didn't lose it, Marylin. I heard it when it fell. Jobs is like vaccination, they take or they don't."

"They never take with you, Getaway."

"Don't you believe it. I'm on one now—"

"A job?"

"Aw, not the way you mean. Me and a guy got a business proposition on. If it goes through, I'll buy you a marriage license engraved on solid gold."

"What is it, then, the proposition?"

"Can't you trust me, Marylin, for a day or two, until it goes through? Sometimes just talking about it is enough to put the jinx on a good thing."

"You mean—"

"I mean I'm going to have money in my pockets."

"What kind of money?"

"Real money."

"*Honest* money?"

"Honest-to-God money. And I'm going to dike you out. That's my idea. Pink! That's the color for you. A pink sash and slippers, and one of them hats that show your yellow hair right through it, and a lace umbrella and—"

"And streamers on the hat! I've always been just crazy for streamers on a hat."

"Red-white-and-blue ones!"

"No, just pink. Wide ones to dangle it like a basket."

"And slippers with real diamond buckles."

"What do you mean, Getaway? How can you give me real diamond shoe buckles—"

"There you go again. Didn't you promise to trust me and my new business proposition?"

"I do, only you've had so many—"

"You do—*only!* Yah, you do, only you don't!"

"I—You see—Getaway—I know how desperate you can be—when you're cornered. I'll never forget how you—you nearly killed a cop—once! Oh, Getaway, when I think back, that time you got into such trouble with—"

"Leave it to a woman, by Jove! to spoil a fellow's good name, if she has to rub her fingers in old soot to do it."

"I—I guess it is from seeing so much around me all the time that it's in me so to suspect."

"Oh, it's in you all right. Gawalmighty knows that!"

"You see, it's because I've seen so much all my life. That's why it's been so grand these last years since I'm alone and—and away from it. Nothing to fear. My own little room and my own little job and me not getting heart failure every time I recognize a plain-clothes man on the beat or hear a night stick on the sidewalk jerk me out of my sleep. Getaway, don't do anything bad. You had one narrow escape. You're finger-printed. Headquarters wouldn't give you the benefit of a doubt if there was one. Don't—Getaway!"

"Yah, stay straight and you'll stay lonesome."

"Money wouldn't make no difference with me, anyway, if everything else wasn't all right. Nothing can be pink to me even if it is pink, unless it's honest. That's why I hold back, Getaway—there's things in you I—can't trust."

"Yah, fine chance of you holding back if I was to come rolling up to your door in a six-cylinder—"

"I tell you, no! If I was that way I wouldn't be holding down the same old job at the factory. I know plenty of boys who turn over easy money. Too easy—"

"Then marry me, Marylin, and you'll wear diamonds. In a couple of days, when this goes through, this deal with the fellows—oh, *honest* deal, if that's what you're opening your mouth to ask—I can stand up beside you with money in my pockets. Twenty bucks to the pastor, just like that! Then you can pick out another job and I'll hold it down for you. Bet your life I will—Oh—here, Marylin—this way—quick!"

"Getaway, why did you turn down this street so all of a sudden? This isn't my way home."

"It's only a block out of the way. Come on! Don't stand gassing."

"You-thought-that-fellow-on-the-corner-of-Dock-Street-might-be-a-plain - clothes-man!"

"What if I did? Want me to go up and kiss him?"

"Why-should-you-care, Getaway?"

"Don't."

"But—"

"Don't believe in hugging the law, though. It's enough when it hugs you."

"I want to go home, Getaway."

"Come on. I'll buy some supper. Steak and French frieds and some French pastry with a cherry on top for your little sweet tooth. That's the kind of a regular guy I am."

"No. I want to go home."

"All right, all right! I'm taking you there, ain't I?"

"Straight."

"Oh, you'll go straight, if you can't go that way anywhere but home."

They trotted the little detour in silence, the corners of her mouth wilting, he would have declared, had he the words, like a field flower in the hands of a picnicker. Marylin could droop that way, so suddenly and so whitely that almost a second could blight her.

"Now you're mad, ain't you?" he said, ashamed to be so quickly conciliatory and trying to make his voice grate.

"No, Getaway—not mad—only I guess—sad."

She stopped before her rooming house. It was as long and as lean and as brown as a witch, and, to the more fanciful, something even of the riding of a broom in the straddle of the doorway, with an empty flagpole jutting from it. And then there was the cat, too—not a black one with gold eyes, just one of the city's myriad of mackerel ones, with chewed ear and a skillful crouch for the leap from ash to garbage can.

"I'm going in now, Getaway."

"Gowann! Get into your blue dress and I'll blow you to supper."

"Not to-night."

"Mad?"

"No. I said only—"

"Sad?"

"No—tired—I guess."

"Please, Marylin."

"No. Some other time."

"When? To-morrow? It's Saturday! Coney?"

"Oh!"

He thought he detected the flash of a dimple. He did. Remember, she was very young and, being fanciful enough to find the witch in the face of her rooming house, the waves at Coney Island, peanut cluttered as they were apt to be, told her things. Silly, unrepeatable things. Nonsense things. Little secret goosefleshing things. Prettinesses. And then the shoot the chutes! That ecstatic leap of heart to lips and the feeling of folly down at the very pit of her. Marylin did like the shoot the chutes!

"All right, Getaway—to-morrow—Coney!"

He did not conceal his surge of pleasure, grasping her small hand in both his. "Good girlie!"

"Good night, Getaway," she said, but with the inflection of something left unsaid.

He felt the unfinished intonation, like a rocket that had never dropped its stick, and started up the steps after her.

"What is it, Marylin?"

"Nothing," she said and ran in.

The window in her little rear room with the zigzag of fire escape across it was already full of dusk. She took off her hat, a black straw with a little pink-cotton rose on it, and, rubbing her brow where it had left a red rut, sat down beside the window. There were smells there from a city bouquet of frying foods; from a pool of old water near a drain pipe; from the rear of a butcher shop. Slops. Noises, too. Babies, traffic, whistles, oaths, barterings, women, strife, life. On her very own ceiling the whisper of footsteps—of restless comings and goings—stealthy comings and goings—and then after an hour, suddenly and ever so softly, the ball-of-a-foot—squeak! The-ball-of-a-foot—squeak!

Marylin knew that step.

And yet she sat, quiet. A star had come out. Looking up at the napkin of sky let in through the walls of the vertical city, Marylin had learned to greet it almost every clear evening. It did something for her. It was a little voice. A little kiss. A little upside down pool of light without a spill. A little of herself up there in that beyond—that little napkin of beyond that her eyes had the lift to see.

* * * * *

Who are you, whose neck has never ached from nine hours a day, six days a week, of bending over the blue-denim pleat that goes down the front of men's shirts, to quiver a supersensitive, supercilious, and superior nose over what, I grant you, may appear on the surface to be the omelet of vulgarities fried up for you on the gladdest, maddest strip of carnival in the world?

But it is simpler to take on the cold glaze of sophistication than to remain simple. When the eyelids become weary, it is as if little red dancing shoes were being wrapped away forever, or a very tight heartstring had suddenly sagged, and when plucked at could no longer plong.

To Marylin, whose neck very often ached clear down into her shoulder blade and up into a bandeau around her brow, and to whom city walls were sometimes like slaps confronting her whichever way she turned, her enjoyment of Coney Island was as uncomplex as A B C. Untortured by any awarenesses of relative values, too simple to strive to keep simple, unself-conscious, and with a hungry heart, she was not a spectator, half ashamed of being amused. She *was* Coney Island! Her heart a shoot the chutes for sheer swoops of joy, her eyes full of confetti points, the surf creaming no higher than her vitality.

And it was so the evening following, as she came dancing down the kicked-up sand of the beach, in a little bright-blue frock, mercerized silk, if you please, with very brief sleeves that ended right up in the jolliest part of her arm, with a half moon of vaccination winking out roguishly beneath a finish of ribbon bow, and a white-canvas sport hat with a jockey rosette to cap the little climax of her, and by no means least, a metal coin purse, with springy insides designed to hold exactly fifty cents in nickels.

Once on the sand, which ran away, tickling each step she took, her spirits, it must be admitted, went just a little crazily off. The window, you see, where Marylin sewed her buttonholes six days the week, faced a brick wall that peeled with an old scrofula of white paint. Coney Island faced a world of sky. So that when she pinched Getaway's nose in between the lips of her coin purse and he, turning a double somersault right in his checked suit, landed seated in a sprawl of mock daze, off she went into peals of laughter only too ready to be released.

He bought her a wooden whirring machine, an instrument of noise that, because it was not utilitarian, became a toy of delicious sound.

They rode imitation ocean waves at five cents a voyage, their only *mal de mer*, regret when it was over. He bought her salt-water taffy, and when the little red cave of her mouth became too ludicrously full of the pully stuff he tried to kiss its state of candy paralysis, and instantly she became sober and would have no more of his nonsense.

"Getaway," she cried, snapping fingers of inspiration, "let's go in bathing!"

"I'll say we will!"

No sooner said than done. In rented bathing suits, unfastidious, if you will, but, pshaw! with the ocean for wash day, who minded! Hers a little blue wrinkly one that hit her far too far, below the knees, but her head flowered up in a polka-dotted turban, that well enough she knew bound her up prettily, and her arms were so round with that indescribable softiness of youth! Getaway, whose eyes could focus a bit when he looked at them, set up a leggy dance at sight of her. He shocked her a bit in his cheap cotton trunks— woman's very old shock to the knobby knees and hairy arms of the beach. But they immediately ran, hand in hand, down the sand and fizz! into the grin of a breaker.

Marylin with her face wet and a fringe of hair, like a streak of seaweed, down her cheek! Getaway, shivery and knobbier than ever, pushing great palms of water at her and she back at him, only less skillfully her five fingers spread and inefficient. Once in the water, he caught and held her close, and yet, for the wonder of it, almost reverentially close, as if what he would claim for himself he must keep intact.

"Marry me, Marylin," he said, with all the hubbub of the ocean about them.

She reached for some foam that hissed out before she could touch it.

"That's you," he said. "Now you are there, and now you aren't."

"I wish," she said—"oh, Getaway, there's so much I wish!"

"What do you wish?"

She looked off toward the immensity of sea and sky. "I—Oh, I don't know! Being here makes me wish—Something as beautiful as out there is what I wish."

"Out where?"

"There."

"I don't see—"

"You—wouldn't."

And then, because neither of them could swim, he began chasing her through shallow water, and in the kicked-up spray of their own merriment they emerged finally, dripping and slinky, the hairs of his forearms lashed flat, and a little drip of salt water running off the tip of her chin.

Until long after the sun went down they lay drying on the sand, her hair spread in a lovely amber flare, and, stretched full length on his stomach beside her, he built a little grave of sand for her feet. And the crowd thinned, and even before the sun dipped a faint young moon, almost as if wearing a veil, came up against the blue. They were quiet now with pleasant fatigue, and, propped up on his elbows, he spilled little rills of sand from one fist into the other.

"Gee! you're pretty, Marylin!"

"Are I, Getaway?"

"You know you are. You wasn't born with one eye shut and the other blind."

"Honest, I don't know. Sometimes I look in the mirror and hope so."

"You've had enough fellows tell you so."

"Yes, but—but not the kind of fellows that mean by pretty what *I* mean by pretty."

"Well, this here guy means what you mean by pretty."

"What do you mean by pretty, Getaway?"

"Pep. Peaches. Cream. Teeth. Yellow hair. Arms. Le—those little holes in your cheeks. Dimples. What do I mean by pretty? I mean you by pretty. Ain't that what you want me to mean by pretty?"

"Yes—and no—"

"Well, what the—"

"It's all right, Getaway. It's fine to be pretty, but—not enough—somehow. I—I can't explain it to you—to anybody. I guess pretty isn't the word. It's beauty I mean."

"All right, then, anything your little heart desires—beauty."

"The ocean beauty out there, I mean. Something that makes you hurt and want to hurt more and more. Beauty, Getaway. It's something you understand or something you don't. It can't be talked. It sounds silly."

"Well, then, whistle it!"

"It has to be *felt*."

"Peel me," he said, laying her arm to his bare bicep. "Some little gladiator, eh? Knock the stuffings out of any guy that tried to take you away from me."

She turned her head on its flare of drying hair away from him. The beach was all but quiet and the haze of the end of day in the air, almost in her eyes, too.

"Oh, Getaway!" she said, on a sigh, and again, "Getaway!"

His reserve with her, at which he himself was the first to marvel, went down a little then and he seized her bare arm, kissing it, almost sinking his teeth. The curve of her chin down into her throat, as she turned her head, had maddened him.

"Quit," she said.

"Never you mind. You'll wear diamonds," he said, in his sole phraseology of promise. "Will you get sore if I ask you something, Fairylin?"

"What?"

"Want one now?"

"Want what?"

"A diamond."

"No," she said. "When I'm out here I quit wanting things like that."

"Fine chance a fellow has to warm up to you!"

"Getaway!"

"What?"

"What did you do last night, after you walked home with me?"

"When?"

"You know when."

"Why, bless your heart, I went home, Fairylin!"

"Please, Getaway—"

"Home, Fairy."

"You were up in Monkey's room last night about eleven. Now think, Getaway!"

"Aw now—"

"You were."

"Aw now—"

"Nobody can fool me on your step. You tiptoed for all you were worth, but I knew it! The-ball-of your-foot—squeak! The-ball-of-your foot—squeak!"

"Sure enough, now you mention it, maybe for a minute around eleven, but only for a minute—"

"Please, Getaway, don't lie. It was for nearly all night. Comings and goings on my ceiling until I couldn't sleep, not because they were so noisy, but because they were so soft. Like ugly whispers. Is Monkey the friend you got the deal on with, Getaway?"

"We just sat up there talking old times—"

"And Muggs, about eleven o'clock, sneaking up through the halls, dressed like the messenger boy again. I saw him when I peeked out of the door to see who it was tiptoeing. Getaway, for God's sake—"

He closed over her wrist then, his face extremely pointed. It was a bony face, so narrow that the eyes and the cheek bones had to be pitched close, and his black hair, usually so shiny, was down in a bang now, because it was damp, and to Marylin there was something sinister in that dip of bang which frightened her.

"What you don't know don't hurt you. You hear that? Didn't I tell you that after a few days this business deal—*business*, get that?—will be over. Then I'm going to hold down any old job your heart desires. But first I'm going to have money in my pockets! That's the only way to make this old world sit up and take notice. Spondulicks! Then I'm going to carry you off and get spliced. See? Real money. Diamonds. If you weren't so touchy, maybe you'd have diamonds sooner than you think. Want one now?"

"Getaway, I know you're up to something. You and Monkey and Muggs are tied up with those Wall Street bond getaways."

"For the luvagod, cut that talk here! First thing I know you'll have me in a brainstorm too."

"Those fake messenger boys that get themselves hired and, instead of delivering the bonds from one office to another—disappear with them. Muggs isn't wearing that messenger's uniform for nothing. You and Monkey are working with him under cover on something. You can't pass a cop any more without tightening up. I can feel it when I have your arm. You've got that old over-your-shoulder look to you, Getaway. My father—had it. My—mother—too. Getaway!"

"By gad! you can't beat a woman!"

"You don't deny it."

"I do!"

"Oh, Getaway, I'm glad then, glad!"

"Over-the-shoulder look. Why, if I'd meet a plain-clothes this minute I'd go up and kiss him—with my teeth in his ear. That's how much I got to be afraid of."

"Oh, Getaway, I'm so glad!"

"Well, then, lay off—"

"Getaway, you jumped then! Like somebody had hit you, and it was only a kid popping a paper bag."

"You get on my nerves. You'd make a cat nervous, with your suspecting! The more a fellow tries to do for a girl like you the less—Look here now, you got to get the hell out of my business."

She did not reply, but lay to the accompaniment of his violent nervousness and pinchings into the sand, with her face still away from him, while the dusk deepened and the ocean quieted.

After a while: "Now, Marylin, don't be sore. I may be a rotten egg some ways, but when it comes to you, I'm there."

"I'm not sore, Getaway," she said, with her voice still away from him. "Only I—Let's not talk for a minute. It's so quiet out here—so full of rest."

He sat, plainly troubled, leaning back on the palms of his hands and dredging his toes into the sand. In the violet light the tender line of her chin to her throat still teased him.

Down farther along the now deserted beach a youth in a bathing suit was playing a harmonica, his knees hunched under his chin, his mouth and hand sliding at cross purposes along the harp. That was the silhouette of him against a clean sky, almost Panlike, as if his feet might be cloven.

What he played, if it had any key at all, was rather in the mood of Chopin's Nocturne in D flat major. A little sigh for the death of a day, a sob for the beauty of that death, and a hope and ecstasy for the new day yet unborn—all of that on a little throbbing mouth organ.

"Getaway," cried Marylin, and sat up, spilling sand, "that's it! That's what I meant a while ago. Hear? It can't be talked. That's it on the mouth organ!"

"It?"

"It! Yes, like I said. Somebody has to feel it inside of him, just like I do, before he can understand. Can't you feel it? Please! Listen."

"Aw, that's an old jew's-harp. I'll buy you one. How's that?"

"All right, I guess," she said, starting off suddenly toward the bathhouse.

He was relieved that she had thrown off the silence.

"Ain't mad any more, are you, Marylin?"

"No, Getaway—not mad."

"Mustn't get fussy that way with me, Marylin. It scares me off. I've had something to show you all day, but you keep scaring me off."

"What is it?" she said, tiptoe.

His mouth drew up to an oblique. "You know."

"No, I don't."

"Maybe I'll tell you and maybe I won't," he cried, scooping up a handful of sand and spraying her. "What'll you give me if I tell?"

"Why—nothing."

"Want to know?"

But at the narrowing something in his eyes she sidestepped him, stooping down at the door of her bathhouse for a last scoop of sand at him.

"No," she cried, her hair blown like spray and the same breeze carrying her laughter, guiltless of mood, out to sea.

On the way home, though, for the merest second, there recurred the puzzling quirk in her thoughtlessness.

In the crush of the electric train, packed tightly into the heart of the most yammering and petulant crowd in the world—home-going pleasure seekers—a youth rose to give her his seat. A big, beach-tanned fellow with a cowlick of hair, when he tipped her his hat, standing up off his right brow like a little apostrophe to him, and blue eyes so very wide apart, and so clear, that they ran back into his head like aisles with little lakes shining at the ends of them.

"Thank you," said Marylin, the infinitesimal second while his hat and cowlick lifted, her own gaze seeming to run down those avenues of his eyes for a look into the pools at the back.

"That was it, too, Getaway! The thing that fellow looked—that I couldn't say. He said it—with his eyes."

"Who?"

"That fellow who gave me this seat."

"I'll break his face if he goo-goos you," said Getaway, who by this time had a headache and whose feet had fitted reluctantly back into patent leather.

But inexplicably, even to herself, that night, in the shadow of the stoop of her witch of a rooming house, she let him kiss her lips. His first of her—her first to any man. It may have been that suddenly she was so extremely tired—tired of the lay of the week ahead, suggested by the smells and the noises and the consciousness of that front box pleat.

The little surrender, even though she drew back immediately, was wine to him and as truly an intoxicant.

"Marylin," he cried, wild for her lips again, "I can't be held off much longer. I'm straight with you, but I'm human, too."

"Don't, Getaway, not here! To-morrow—maybe."

"I'm crazy for you!"

"Go home now, Getaway."

"Yes—but just one more—"

"Promise me you'll go straight home from here—to bed."

"I promise. Marylin, one more. One little more. Your lips—"

"No, no—not now. Go—"

Suddenly, by a quirk in the dark, there was a flash of something down Marylin's bare third finger, so hurriedly and so rashly that it scraped the flesh.

"That's for you! I've been afraid all day. Touchy! Didn't I tell you? Diamonds! Now will you kiss me? Now will you?"

In the shadow of where she stood, looking down, it was as if she gazed into a pool of fire that was reaching in flame clear up about her head, and everywhere in the conflagration Getaway's triumphant "Now will you! Now will you!"

"Getaway," she cried, flecking her hand as if it burned, "where did you get this?"

"It's for you, Fairylin, and more like it coming. It weighs a carat and a half. That stone's worth more than a sealskin jacket. You're going to have one of those, too. Real seal! Now are you sore at me any more? Now you've a swell kick coming, haven't you? Now! Now!"

"Getaway," she cried behind her lit hand, because her palm was to her mouth and above it her eyes showing the terror in their whites, "where did you get this?"

"There!" he said, and kissed her hotly and squarely on the lips.

Somehow, with the ring off her finger and in a little pool of its light as it lay at his feet, where he stood dazed on the sidewalk, Marylin was up the stoop, through the door, up two flights, and through her own door, slamming it, locking it, and into her room, rubbing and half crying over her left third finger where the flash had been.

She was frightened, because for all of an hour she sat on the end of the cot in her little room trembling and with her palms pressed into her eyes so tightly that the darkness spun. There was quick connection in Marylin between what was emotional and what was merely sensory. She knew, from the sickness at the very pit of her, how sick were her heart and her soul— and how afraid.

She undressed in the dark—a pale darkness relieved by a lighted window across the areaway. The blue mercerized dress she slid over a hanger, covering it with one of her cotton nightgowns and putting it into careful place behind the cretonne curtain that served her as clothes closet. Her petticoat, white, with a rill of lace, she folded away. And then, in her bare feet and a pink-cotton nightgown with a blue bird machine-stitched on the yoke, stood cocked to the hurry of indistinct footsteps across her ceiling, and in the narrow slit of hallway outside her door, where the stairs led up still another flight, the-ball-of-a-foot—squeak! The sharp crack of a voice. Running.

"Getaway!" cried Marylin's heart, almost suffocating her with a dreadful spasm of intuition.

It was all so quick. In the flash of her flung-open door, as her head in its amber cloud leaned out, Getaway, bending almost double over the upper banister, his lips in his narrow face back to show a white terribleness of strain that lingered in the memory, hurled out an arm suddenly toward two men mounting the steps of the flight below him.

There was a shot then, and on the lower flight one of the men, with an immediate red mouth opening slowly in his neck, slid downstairs backward, face up.

Suddenly, from a crouching position beside her door, the second figure shot forward now, with ready and perfect aim at the already-beginning-to-be-nerveless figure of Getaway hanging over the banister with the smoking pistol.

By the reaching out of her right hand Marylin could have deflected that perfect aim. In fact, her arm sprang toward just that reflex act, then stayed itself with the jerk of one solid body avoiding collision with another.

So much quicker than it takes in the telling there marched across Marylin's sickened eyes this frieze: Her father trailing dead from the underslinging of a freight car. That moment when a uniform had stepped in from the fire escape across the bolt of Brussels lace; her mother's scream, like a plunge into the heart of a rapier. Uniforms—contemplating. On street corners. Opposite houses. Those four fingers peeping over each of her father's shoulders in the courtroom. Getaway! His foxlike face leaner. Meaner. Black mask. Electric chair. Volts. Ugh—volts! God—you know—best—help—

When the shot came that sent Getaway pitching forward down the third-floor flight she was on her own room floor in a long and merciful faint. Marylin had not reached out.

* * * * *

Time passed. Whole rows of days of buttonholes down pleats that were often groped at through tears. Heavy tears like magnifying glasses. And then, with that gorgeous and unassailable resiliency of youth, lighter tears. Fewer tears. Few tears. No tears.

Under the cretonne curtain, though, the blue mercerized frock hung unworn, and in its dark drawer remained the petticoat with its rill of lace. But one night, with a little catch in her throat (it was the last of her sobs), she took out the sport hat, and for no definite reason began to turn the jockey rosette to the side where the sun had not faded it.

These were quiet evenings in her small room. All the ceiling agitation had long ago ceased since the shame of the raided room above, and Muggs, in his absurd messenger's suit, and Monkey marching down the three flights to the clanking of steel at the wrists.

There were new footsteps now. Steps that she had also learned to know, but pleasantly. They marched out so regularly of mornings, invariably just as she was about to hook her skirtband or pull on her stockings. They came home so patly again at seven, about as she sat herself down to a bit of sewing or washing-out. They went to bed so pleasantly. Thud, on the floor, and then, after the expectant interval of unlacing, thud again. They were companionable, those footsteps, almost like reverential marching on the grave of her heart.

Marylin reversed the rosette, and as the light began to go sat down beside her window, idly, looking up. There was the star point in her patch of sky, eating its way right through the purple like a diamond, and her ache over it was so tangible that it seemed to her she could almost lift the hurt out of her heart, as if it were a little imprisoned bird. And as it grew darker there came two stars, and three, and nine, and finally the sixty hundred.

Then from the zig of the fire escape above, before it twisted down into the zag of hers, there came to Marylin, through the medley of city silences and the tears in her heart, this melody, on a jew's-harp:

If it had any key at all, it was in the mood of Chopin's Nocturne in D flat major. A little sigh for the death of a day, a sob for the beauty of that death, and the throb of an ecstasy for the new day not yet born.

Looking up against the sheer wall of the vertical city, on the ledge of fire escape above hers, and in the yellow patch of light thrown out from the room behind, a youth, with his knees hunched up under his chin, and his mouth and hand moving at cross purposes, was playing the harmonica.

Wide apart were his eyes, and blue, so that while she gazed up, smiling, as he gazed down, smiling, it was almost as if she ran up the fire escape through the long clear lanes of those eyes, for a dip into the little twin lakes at the back of them.

And—why, didn't you know?—there was a lift of cowlick to the right side of his front hair, as he sat there playing in the twilight, that was exactly the shape of an apostrophe!

THE SMUDGE

In the bleak little graveyard of Hattie Bertch's dead hopes, dead loves, and dead ecstasies, more than one headstone had long since begun to sag and the wreaths of bleeding heart to shrivel.

That was good, because the grave that is kept bubbly with tears is a tender, quivering thing, almost like an amputated bit of self that still aches with threads of life.

Even over the mound of her dead ambitions, which grave she had dug with the fingers of her heart, Hattie could walk now with unsensitive feet. It had become dry clay with cracks in it like sardonic smiles.

Smiles. That was the dreadful part, because the laugh where there have been tears is not a nice laugh, and Hattie could sit among the headstones of her dead dreams now and laugh. But not horridly. Just drearily.

There was one grave, Heart's Desire, that was still a little moist. But it, too, of late years, had begun to sink in, like an old mouth with receding gums, as if the very teeth of a smiling dream had rotted. They had.

Hattie, whose heart's desire had once been to play Juliet, played maids now. Buxom negro ones, with pale palms, white eyes, and the beat of kettledrums somewhere close to the cuticle of the balls of her feet.

She was irrevocably down on managers' and agents' lists as "comedy black." Countless the premiers she had opened to the fleck of a duster! Hattie came high, as maids go. One hundred and fifty dollars a week and no road engagements. She dressed alone. Her part in "Love Me Long" had been especially written in for the sake of the peculiar kind of comedy relief she could bring to it. A light roar of recognition swept the audience at her entrance. Once in a while, a handclap. So Hattie, whose heart's desire had once been to play Juliet, played maids now. Buxomly.

And this same Hattie, whose heart's desire had once been to kiss Love, but whose lips were still a little twisted with the taste of clay, could kiss only Love's offspring now. But not bitterly. Thanksgivingly.

Love's offspring was Marcia. Sixteen and the color and odor of an ivory fan that has lain in frangipani. And Hattie could sometimes poke her tongue into her cheek over this bit of whimsy:

It was her well-paid effort in the burnt cork that made possible, for instance, the frill of real lace that lay to the low little neck of Marcia's first party dress, as if blown there in sea spume.

Out of the profits of Hattie's justly famous Brown Cold Cream—Guaranteed Color-fast—Mulatto, Medium, Chocolate, had come Marcia's ermine muff and tippet; the enamel toilet set; the Steinway grand piano; the yearly and by no means light tuition toll at Miss Harperly's Select Day School for Girls.

You get the whimsy of it? For everything fair that was Marcia, Hattie had brownly paid for. Liltingly, and with the rill of the song of thanksgiving in her heart.

That was how Hattie moved through her time. Hugging this melody of Marcia. Through the knife-edged nervous evenings in the theater. Bawlings. Purple lips with loose muscles crawling under the rouge. Fetidness of scent on stale bodies. Round faces that could hook into the look of vultures when the smell of success became as the smell of red meat. All the petty soiled vanities, like the disordered boudoir of a cocotte. The perpetual stink of perfume. Powder on the air and caking the breathing. Open dressing-room doors that should have been closed. The smelling geometry of the make-up box. Curls. Corsets. Cosmetics. Men in undershirts, grease-painting. "Gawdalmighty, Tottie, them's my teddy bears you're puttin' on." Raw nerves. Raw emotions. Ego, the actor's overtone, abroad everywhere and full of strut. "Overture!" The wait in the wings. Dizziness at the pit of the stomach. Audiences with lean jaws etched into darkness. Jaws that can smile or crack your bones and eat you. Faces swimming in the stage ozone and wolfish for cue. The purple lips—

Almost like a frieze stuck on to the border of each day was Hattie's life in the theater. Passementerie.

That was how Hattie treated it. Especially during those placid years of the phenomenal New York run of "Love Me Long." The outer edge of her reality. The heart of her reality? Why, the heart of it was the long morning hours in her own fragrant kitchen over doughnuts boiled in oil and snowed under in powdered sugar! Cookies that bit with a snap. Filet of sole boned with fingers deft at it and served with a merest fluff of tartar sauce. Marcia ate like that. Preciously. Pecksniffily. An egg at breakfast a gag to the sensibilities! So Hattie ate hers in the kitchen, standing, and tucked the shell out of sight, wrapped in a lettuce leaf. Beefsteak, for instance, sickened Marcia, because there was blood in the ooze of its juices. But Hattie had a sly way of camouflage. Filet mignon (so strengthening, you see) crushed under a little millinery of mushrooms and served under glass. Then when Marcia's neat little row of neat little teeth bit in and the munch began behind clean and careful lips, Hattie's heart, a regular old bandit for cunning, beat hoppity, skippity, jump!

Those were her realities. Home. The new sandwich cutters. Heart shape. Diamond shape. Spade. The strip of hall carpet newly discovered to scour like new with brush and soap and warm water. Epstein's meat market throws in free suet. The lamp with the opal-silk shade for Marcia's piano. White oilcloth is cleaner than shelf paper. Dotted Swiss curtains, the ones in Marcia's room looped back with pink bows. Old sashes, pressed out and fringed at the edges.

And if you think that Hattie's six rooms and bath and sunny, full-sized kitchen, on Morningside Heights, were trumped-up ones of the press agent for the Sunday Supplement, look in.

Any afternoon. Tuesday, say, and Marcia just home from school. On Tuesday afternoon of every other week Hattie made her cream, in a large copper pot that hung under the sink. Six dozen half-pint jars waiting to be filled with Brown Cold Cream. One hundred and forty-four jars a month. Guaranteed Color-fast. Mulatto, Medium, Chocolate. Labeled. Sealed. Sold. And demand exceeding the supply. An ingratiating, expert cream, known the black-faced world over. It slid into the skin, not sootily, but illuminating it to winking, African copper. For instance, Hattie's make-up cream for Linda in "Love Me Long" was labeled "Chocolate." But it worked in even a truer brown, as if it had come out of the pigment instead of gone into the pores.

Four hours of stirring it took, adding with exact minutiae the mysteriously proper proportions of spermacetti, oil of sweet almonds, white wax—But never mind. Hattie's dark secret was her own.

Fourteen years of her black art as Broadway's maid *de luxe* had been her laboratory. It was almost her boast now—remember the sunken headstones—that she had handled spotlessly every fair young star of the theaters' last ten years.

It was as mysterious as pigment, her cream, and as true, and netted her, with occasional extra batches, an average of two hundred dollars a month. She enjoyed making it. Singing as she stirred or rather stirring as she sang, the plenitude of her figure enveloped in a blue-and-white bungalow apron with rickrack trimming.

Often Marcia, home from day school, watched. Propped up in the window frame with her pet cat, a Persian, with eyes like swimming pools with painted green bottoms, seated in a perfect circle in her quiet lap, for all the world in the attitude of a sardel except for the toothpick through.

Sometimes it almost seemed as if Marcia did the purring. She could sit like that, motionless, her very stare seeming to sleep. To Hattie that stare was beautiful, and in a way it was. As if two blue little suns were having their high noon.

Sometimes Marcia offered to help, because toward the end, Hattie's back could ache at this process, terribly, the pain knotting itself into her face when the rotary movement of her stirring arm began to yank at her nerves.

"Momie, I'll stir for a while."

Marcia's voice was day-schooled. As clipped, as boxed, and as precise as a hedge. Neat, too, as neat as the way her clear lips met, and her teeth, which had a little mannerism of coming down after each word, biting them off like threads. They were appealing teeth that had never grown big or square. Very young corn. To Hattie there was something about them that reminded her of a tiny set of Marcia's doll dishes that she had saved. Little innocences.

"I don't mind stirring, dear. I'm not tired."

"But your face is all twisted."

Hattie's twisted face could induce in Marcia the same gagged pallor that the egg in the morning or the red in the beefsteak juices brought there.

"Go in and play the piano awhile, Marcy, I'll be finished soon."

"Sh-h-h! No. Pussy-kitty's asleep."

As the cream grew heavier and its swirl in the pot slower, Hattie could keep the twist out of her face only by biting her tongue. She did, and a little arch of sweat came out in a mustache.

The brown mud of the cream began to fluff. Hattie rubbed a fleck of it into her freckled forearm. Yes, Hattie's arm was freckled, and so was the bridge of her nose, in a little saddle. Once there had been a prettiness to the freckles because they whitened the skin they sprinkled and were little stars to the moon reddiness of Hattie's hair. But the red of the moon had set coldly in Hattie's hair now, and the stars were just freckles, and there was the dreaded ridge of flesh showing above the ridge of her corsets, and when she leaned forward to stir her cheeks hung forward like a spaniel's, not of fat, but heaviness. Hattie's arms and thighs were granite to the touch and to the scales. Kindly freckled granite. She weighed almost twice what she looked. Marcia, whose hips were like lyres, hated the ridge above the corset line and massaged it. Mab smacking the Himalayas.

After a while, there in the window frame, Marcia closed her eyes. There was still the illusion of a purr about her. Probably because, as her kitten warmed in its circle, its coziness began to whir mountingly. The September afternoon was full of drone. The roofs of the city from Hattie's kitchen window, which overlooked Morningside Heights, lay flat as slaps. Tranced, indoor quiet. Presently Hattie began to tiptoe. The seventy-two jars were untopped now, in a row on a board over the built-in washtub. Seventy-two yawning for content. Squnch! Her enormous spoon into the copper kettle and flop, gurgle, gooze, softly into the jars. One—two—three—At the sixty-eighth, Marcia, without stirring or lifting her lids, spoke into the sucky silence.

"Momie?"

"Yes, Marcy."

"You'll be glad."

Hattie, pausing at the sixty-eighth, "Why, dear?"

"I came home in Nonie Grosbeck's automobile. I'm invited to a dinner dance October the seventeenth. At their house in Gramercy Park."

The words must have gone to Hattie's knees, because, dropping a spat of mulatto cold cream on the linoleum, she sat down weakly on the kitchen chair that she had painted blue and white to match the china cereal set on the shelf above it.

"Marcy!"

"And she likes me better than any girl in school, momie, and I'm to be her chum from to-day on, and not another girl in school is invited except Edwina Nelson, because her father's on nearly all the same boards of directors with Mr. Grosbeck, and—"

"Marcia! Marcia! and you came home from school just as if nothing had happened! Child, sometimes I think you're made of ice."

"Why, I'm glad, momie."

But that's what there were, little ice glints of congealed satisfaction in Marcia's eyes.

"Glad," said Hattie, the word full of tears. "Why, honey, you don't realize it, but this is the beginning! This is the meaning of my struggle to get you into Miss Harperly's school. It wasn't easy. I've never told you the—strings I had to pull. Conservative people, you see. That's what the Grosbecks are, too. Home people. The kind who can afford to wear dowdy hats and who have lived in the same house for thirty years."

"Nome's mother was born in the house they live in."

"Substantial people, who half-sole their shoes and endow colleges. Taxpayers. Policyholders. Church members. Oh, Marcia, those are the safe people!"

"There's a Grosbeck memorial window in the Rock Church."

"I used to be so afraid for you, Marcy. Afraid you would take to the make-believe folks. The play people. The theater. I used to fear for you! The Pullman car. The furnished room. That going to the hotel room, alone, nights after the show. You laugh at me sometimes for just throwing a veil over my face and coming home black-face. It's because I'm too tired, Marcy. Too lonesome for home. On the road I always used to think of all the families in the audience. The husbands and wives. Brides and grooms. Sweethearts. After the performance they all went to homes. To brownstone fronts like the Grosbecks'. To cottages. To flats. With a snack to eat in the refrigerator or laid out on the dining-room table. Lamps burning and waiting. Nighties laid out and bedcovers turned back. And then—me. Second-rate hotels. That walk through the dark downtown streets. Passing men who address you through closed lips. The dingy lobby. There's no applause lasts long enough, Marcia, to reach over that moment when you unlock your hotel room and the smell of disinfectant and unturned mattress comes out to you."

"Ugh!"

"Oh, keep to the safe people, Marcia! The unexciting people, maybe, but the safe home-building ones with old ideals and old hearthstones."

"Nonie says they have one in their library that comes from Italy."

"Hitch your ideal to a hearthstone like that, Marcia."

"Nonie goes to riding academy."

"So shall you."

"It's six dollars an hour."

"I don't care."

"Her father's retired except for being director in banks. And, momie—they don't mind, dear—about us. Nonie knows that my—father is—is separated and never lived at home with us. She's broad-minded. She says just so there's no scandal, a divorce, or anything like that. She said it's vulgar to cultivate only rich friends. She says she'd go with me even if she's forbidden to."

"Why, Marcy darling, why should she be forbidden?"

"Oh, Nonie's broadminded. She says if two people are unsuited they should separate, quietly, like you and my father. She knows we're one of the first old Southern families on my father's side. I—I'm not trying to make you talk about it, dear, but—but we are—aren't we?"

"Yes, Marcy."

"He—he was just—irresponsible. That's not being—not nice people, is it?"

"No, Marcy."

"Nonie's not forbidden. She just meant in case, momie. You see, with some old families like hers—the stage—but Nonie says her father couldn't even say anything to that if he wanted to. His own sister went on the stage once, and they had to hush it up in the papers."

"Did you explain to her, Marcy, that stage life at its best can be full of fine ideals and truth? Did you make her see how regular your own little life has been? How little you know about—my work? How away I've kept you? How I won't even play out-of-town engagements so we can always be together in our little home? You must explain all those things to your friends at Miss Harperly's. It helps—with steady people."

"I have, momie, and she's going to bring me home every afternoon in their automobile after we've called for her brother Archie at Columbia Law School."

"Marcy! the Grosbeck automobile bringing you home every day!"

"And it's going to call for me the night of the party. Nonie's getting a lemon taffeta."

"I'll get you ivory, with a bit of real lace!"

"Oh, momie, momie, I can scarcely wait!"

"What did she say, Marcy, when she asked—invited you?"

"She?"

"Nonie."

"Why—she—didn't invite me, momie."

"But you just said—"

"It was her brother Archie invited me. We called for him at Columbia Law School, you see. It was he invited me. Of course Nonie wants me and said 'Yes' right after him—but it's he—who wants Nonie and me to be chums. I—He—I thought—I—told—you—momie."

Suddenly Marcia's eyes, almost with the perpendicular slits of her kitten's in them, seemed to swish together like portières, shutting Hattie behind them with her.

"Oh—my Marcy!" said Hattie, dimly, after a while, as if from their depths. "Marcy, dearest!"

"At—at Harperly's, momie, almost all the popular upper-class girls wear—a—a boy's fraternity pin."

"Fraternity pin?"

"It's the—the beginning of being engaged."

"But, Marcy—"

"Archie's a Pi Phi!"

"A—what?"

"A Pi Phi."

"Phi—pie—Marcy—dear—"

* * * * *

On October 17th "Love Me Long" celebrated its two-hundredth performance. Souvenir programs. A few appropriate words by the management. A flashlight of the cast. A round of wine passed in the after-the-performance gloom of the wings. Aqueous figures fading off in the orderly back-stage fashion of a well-established success.

Hattie kissed the star. They liked each other with the unenvy of their divergent roles. Miss Robinson even humored some of Hattie's laughs. She liked to feel the flame of her own fairness as she stood there waiting for the audience to guffaw its fill of Hattie's drolleries; a narcissus swaying reedily beside a black crocodile.

She was a new star and her beauty the color of cloth of gold, and Hattie in her lowly comedian way not an undistinguished veteran. So they could kiss in the key of a cat cannot unseat a king.

But, just the same, Miss Robinson's hand flew up automatically against the dark of Hattie's lips.

"I don't fade off, dearie. Your own natural skin is no more color-fast. I handled Elaine Doremus in 'The Snowdrop' for three seasons. Never so much as a speck or a spot on her. My cream don't fade."

"Of course not, dear! How silly of me! Kiss me again."

That was kind enough of her. Oh yes, they got on. But sometimes Hattie, seated among her sagging headstones, would ache with the dry sob of the black crocodile who yearned toward the narcissus....

Quite without precedent, there was a man waiting for her in the wings.

The gloom of back-stage was as high as trees and Hattie had not seen him in sixteen years. But she knew. With the stunned consciousness of a stabbed person that glinting instant before the blood begins to flow.

It was Morton Sebree—Marcia's father.

"Morton!"

"Hattie."

"Come up to my dressing room," she said, as matter-of-factly as if her brain were a clock ticking off the words.

They walked up an iron staircase of unreality. Fantastic stairs. Wisps of gloom. Singing pains in her climbing legs like a piano key hit very hard and held down with a pressing forefinger. She could listen to her pain. That was her thought as she climbed. How the irrelevant little ideas would slide about in her sudden chaos. She must concentrate now. Terribly. Morton was back.

His hand, a smooth glabrous one full of clutch, riding up the banister. It could have been picked off, finger by finger. It was that kind of a hand. But after each lift, another finger would have curled back again. Morton's hand, ascending the dark like a soul on a string in a burlesque show.

Face to face. The electric bulb in her dressing room was incased in a wire like a baseball mask. A burning prison of light. Fat sticks of grease paint with the grain of Hattie's flesh printed on the daub end. Furiously brown cheesecloth. An open jar of cream (chocolate) with the gesture of the gouge in it. A woolly black wig on a shelf, its kinks seeming to crawl. There was a rim of Hattie *au natural* left around her lips. It made of her mouth a comedy blubber, her own rather firm lips sliding about somewhere in the lightish swamp. That was all of Hattie that looked out. Except her eyes. They were good gray eyes with popping whites now, because of a trick of blackening the lids. But the irises were in their pools, inviolate.

"Well, Hattie, I reckon I'd have known you even under black."

"I thought you were in Rio."

"Got to hankering after the States, Hattie."

"I read of a Morris Sebree died in Brazil. Sometimes I used to think maybe it might have been a misprint—and—that—you—were—the—one."

"No, no. 'Live and kickin'. Been up around here a good while."

"Where?"

"Home. N'Orleans. M' mother died, Hattie, God rest her bones. Know it?"

"No."

"Cancer."

It was a peculiar silence. A terrible word like that was almost slowly soluble in it. Gurgling down.

"O-oh!"

"Sort of gives a fellow the shivers, Hattie, seeing you kinda hidin' behind yourself like this. But I saw you come in the theater to-night. You looked right natural. Little heavier."

"What do you want?"

"Why, I guess a good many things in general and nothing in particular, as the sayin' goes. You don't seem right glad to see me, honey."

"Glad!" said Hattie, and laughed as if her mirth were a dice shaking in a box of echoes.

"Your hair's right red yet. Looked mighty natural walkin' into the theater to-night. Take off those kinks, honey."

She reached for her cleansing cream, then stopped, her eyes full of the foment of torture.

"What's my looks to you?"

"You've filled out."

"You haven't," she said, putting down the cold-cream jar. "You haven't aged an hour. Your kind lies on life like it was a wall in the sun. A wall that somebody else has built for you stone by stone."

"I reckon you're right in some ways, Hattie. There's been a meanderin' streak in me somewheres. You and m' mother, God rest her bones, had a different way of scoldin' me for the same thing. Lot o' Huck Finn in me."

"Don't use bad-boy words for vicious, bad-man deeds!"

"But you liked me. Both of you liked me, honey. Only two women I ever really cared for, too. You and m' mother."

Her face might have been burning paper, curling her scorn for him.

"Don't try that, Morton. It won't work any more. What used to infatuate me only disgusts me now. The things I thought I—loved—in you, I loathe now. The kind of cancer that killed your mother is the kind that eats out the heart. I never knew her, never even saw her except from a distance, but I know, just as well as if I'd lived in that fine big house with her all those years in New Orleans, that you were the sickness that ailed her—lying, squandering, gambling, no-'count son! If she and I are the only women you ever cared for, thank God that there aren't any more of us to suffer from you. Morton, when I read that a Morris Sebree had died in Brazil, I hoped it was you! You're no good! You're no good!"

She was thumping now with the sobs she kept under her voice.

"Why, Hattie," he said, his drawl not quickened, "you don't mean that!"

"I do! You're a ruiner of lives! Her life! Mine! You're a rotten apple that can speck every one it touches."

"That's hard, Hattie, but I reckon you're not all wrong."

"Oh, that softy Southern talk won't get us anywhere, Morton. The very sound of it sickens me now. You're like a terrible sickness I once had. I'm cured now. I don't know what you want here, but whatever it is you might as well go. I'm cured!"

He sat forward in his chair, still twirling the soft brown hat. He was dressed like that. Softly. Good-quality loosely woven stuffs. There was still a tan down of persistent youth on the back of his neck. But his hands were old, the veins twisted wiring, and his third finger yellowly stained, like meerschaum darkening.

"Grantin' everything you say, Hattie—and I'm holdin' no brief for myself—*I've* been the sick one, not you. Twenty years I've been down sick with hookworm."

"With devilishness."

"No, Hattie. It's the government's diagnosis. Hookworm. Been a sick man all my life with it. Funny thing, though, all those years in Rio knocked it out of me."

"Faugh!"

"I'm a new man since I'm well of it."

"Hookworm! That's an easy word for ingrained no-'countness, deviltry, and deceit. It wasn't hookworm came into the New Orleans stock company where I was understudying leads and getting my chance to play big things. It wasn't hookworm put me in a position where I had to take anything I could get! So that instead of finding me playing leads you find me here—black-face! It was a devil! A liar! A spendthrift, no-'count son out of a family that deserved better. I've cried more tears over you than I ever thought any woman ever had it in her to cry. Those months in that boarding house in Peach Tree Street down in New Orleans! Peach Tree Street! I remember how beautiful even the name of it was when you took me there—lying—and how horrible it became to me. Those months when I used to see your mother's carriage drive by the house twice a day and me crying my eyes out behind the curtains. That's what I've never forgiven myself for. She was a woman who stood for fine things in New Orleans. A good woman whom the whole town pitied! A no-'count son squandering her fortune and dragging down the family name. If only I had known all that then! She would have helped me if

I had appealed to her. She wouldn't have let things turn out secretly—the way they did. She would have helped me. I—You—Why have you come here to jerk knives out of my heart after it's got healed with the points sticking in? You're nothing to me. You're skulking for a reason. You've been hanging around, getting pointers about me. My life is my own! You get out!"

"The girl. She well?"

It was a quiet question, spoken in the key of being casual, and Hattie, whose heart skipped a beat, tried to corral the fear in her eyes to take it casually, except that her eyelids seemed to grow old even as they drooped. Squeezed grape skins.

"You get out, Morton," she said. "You've got to get out."

He made a cigarette in an old, indolent way he had of wetting it with his smile. He was handsome enough after his fashion, for those who like the rather tropical combination of dark-ivory skin, and hair a lighter shade of tan. It did a curious thing to his eyes. Behind their allotment of tan lashes they became neutralized. Straw colored.

"She's about sixteen now. Little over, I reckon."

"What's that to you?"

"Blood, Hattie. Thick."

"What thickened it, Morton—after sixteen years?"

"Used to be an artist chap down in Rio. On his uppers. One night, according to my description of what I imagined she looked like, he drew her. Yellow hair, I reckoned, and sure enough—"

"You're not worthy of the resemblance. It wouldn't be there if I had the saying."

"You haven't," he said, suddenly, his teeth snapping together as if biting off a thread.

"Nor you!" something that was the whiteness of fear lightening behind her mask. She rose then, lifting her chair out of the path toward the door and flinging her arm out toward it, very much after the manner of Miss Robinson in Act II.

"You get out, Morton," she said, "before I have you put out. They're closing the theater now. Get out!"

"Hattie," his calm enormous, "don't be hasty. A man that has come to his senses has come back to you humble and sincere. A man that's been sick. Take me back, Hattie, and see if—"

"Back!" she said, lifting her lips scornfully away from touching the word. "You remember that night in that little room on Peach Tree Street when I prayed on my knees and kissed—your—shoes and crawled for your mercy to stay for Marcia to be born? Well, if you were to lie on this floor and kiss my shoes and crawl for my mercy I'd walk out on you the way you walked out on me. If you don't go, I'll call a stage hand and make you go. There's one coming down the corridor now and locking the house. You go—or I'll call!"

His eyes, with their peculiar trick of solubility in his color scheme, seemed all tan.

"I'll go," he said, looking slim and Southern, his imperturbability ever so slightly unfrocked—"I'll go, but you're making a mistake, Hattie."

Fear kept clanging in her. Fire bells of it.

"Oh, but that's like you, Morton! Threats! But, thank God, nothing you can do can harm me any more."

"I reckon she's considerable over sixteen now. Let's see—"

Fire bells. Fire bells.

"Come out with what you want, Morton, like a man! You're feeling for something. Money? Now that your mother is dead and her fortune squandered, you've come to harass me? That's it! I know you, like a person who has been disfigured for life by burns knows fire. Well, I won't pay!"

"Pay? Why, Hattie—I want you—back—"

She could have cried because, as she sat there blackly, she was sick with his lie.

"I'd save a dog from you."

"Then save—her—from me."

The terrible had happened so quietly. Morton had not raised his voice; scarcely his lips.

She closed the door then and sat down once more, but that which had crouched out of their talk was unleashed now.

"That's just exactly what I intend to do."

"How?"

"By saving her sight or sound of you."

"You can't, Hattie."

"Why?"

"I've come back." There was a curve to his words that hooked into her heart like forceps about a block of ice. But she outstared him, holding her lips in the center of the comedy rim so that he could see how firm their bite.

"Not to me."

"To her, then."

"Even you wouldn't be low enough to let her know—"

"Know what?"

"Facts."

"You mean she doesn't know?"

"Know! Know you for what you are and for what you made of me? I've kept it something decent for her. Just the separation of husband and wife—who couldn't agree. Incompatibility. I have not told her—" And suddenly could have rammed her teeth into the tongue that had betrayed her. Simultaneously with the leap of light into his eyes came the leap of her error into her consciousness.

"Oh," he said, and smiled, a slow smile that widened as leisurely as sorghum in the pouring.

"You made me tell you that! You came here for that. To find out!"

"Nothin' the sort, Hattie. You only verified what I kinda suspected. Naturally, you've kept it from her. Admire you for it."

"But I lied! See! I know your tricks. She does know you for what you are and what you made of me. She knows everything. Now what are you going to do? She knows! I lied! I—" then stopped, at the curve his lips were taking and at consciousness of the pitiableness of her device.

"Morton," she said, her hands opening into her lap into pads of great pink helplessness, "you wouldn't tell her—on me! You're not that low!"

"Wouldn't tell what?"

He was rattling her, and so she fought him with her gaze, trying to fasten and fathom under the flicker of his lids. But there were no eyes there. Only the neutral, tricky tan.

"You see, Morton, she's just sixteen. The age when it's more important than anything else in the world to a young girl that's been reared like her to—to have her life *regular*! Like all her other little school friends. She's like that, Morton. Sensitive! Don't touch her, Morton. For God's sake, don't! Some day when she's past having to care so terribly—when she's older—you can rake it up if you must torture. I'll tell her then. But for God's sake, Morton, let us live—now!"

"Hattie, you meet me to-morrow morning and take a little journey to one of these little towns around here in Jersey or Connecticut, and your lie to her won't be a lie any more."

"Morton—I—I don't understand. Why?"

"I'll marry you."

"You fool!" she said, almost meditatively. "So you've heard we've gotten on a bit. You must even have heard of this"—placing her hand over the jar of the Brown Cold Cream. "You want to be in at the feast. You're so easy to read that I can tell you what you're after before you can get the coward words out. Marry you! You fool!"

It was as if she could not flip the word off scornfully enough, sucking back her lower lip, then hurling.

"Well, Hattie," he said, unbunching his soft hat, "I reckon that's pretty plain."

"I reckon it is, Morton."

"All right. Everybody to his own notion of carryin' a grudge to the grave. But it's all right, honey. No hard feelin's. It's something to know I was willin' to do the right thing. There's a fruit steamer out of here for N'Orleans in the mawnin'. Reckon I'll catch it."

"I'd advise you to."

"No objection to me droppin' around to see the girl first? Entitled to a little natural curiosity. Come, I'll take you up home this evenin'. The girl. No harm."

"You're not serious, Morton. You wouldn't upset things. You wouldn't tell—that—child!"

"Why, not in a thousand years, honey, unless you forced me to it. Well, you've forced me. Come, Hattie, I'm seein' you home this evenin'."

"You can't put your foot—"

"Come now. You're too clever a woman to try to prevent me. Course there's a way to keep me from goin' up home with you this evenin'. I wouldn't use it, if I were you. You know I'll get to see her. I even know where she goes to school. Mighty nice selection you made, Hattie, Miss Harperly's."

"You can't frighten me," she said, trying to moisten her lips with her tongue. But it was dry as a parrot's. It was hard to close her lips. They were oval and suddenly immobile as a picture frame. What if she could not swallow. There was nothing to swallow! Dry tongue. O God! Marcia!

That was the fleeting form her panic took, but almost immediately she could manage her lips again. Her lips, you see, they counted so! She must keep them firm in the slippery shine of the comedy black.

"Come," he said, "get your make-up off. I'll take you up in a cab."

"How do you know it's—up?"

"Why, I don't know as I do know exactly. Just came kind of natural to put it that way. Morningside Heights is about right, I calculate."

"So—you *have*—been watching."

"Well, I don't know as I'd put it thataway. Naturally, when I got to town— first thing I did—most natural thing in the world. That's a mighty fine car with a mighty fine-looking boy and a girl brings your—our girl home every afternoon about four. We used to have a family of Grosbeaks down home. Another branch, I reckon."

"O—God!" A malaprop of a tear, too heavy to wink in, came rolling suddenly down Hattie's cheek. "Morton—let—us—live—for God's sake! Please!"

He regarded the clean descent of the tear down Hattie's color-fast cheek and its clear drop into the bosom of her black-taffeta housemaid's dress.

"By Jove! The stuff *is* color-fast! You've a fortune in that cream if you handle it right, honey."

"My way is the right way for me."

"But it's a woman's way. Incorporate. Manufacture it. Get a man on the job. Promote it!"

"Ah, that sounds familiar. The way you promoted away every cent of your mother's fortune until the bed she died in was mortgaged. One of your wildcat schemes again! Oh, I watched you before I lost track of you in South America—just the way you're watching—us—now! I know the way you squandered your mother's fortune. The rice plantation in Georgia. The alfalfa ranch. The solid-rubber-tire venture in Atlanta. You don't get your hands on my affairs. My way suits me!"

The tumult in her was so high and her panic so like a squirrel in the circular frenzy of its cage that she scarcely noted the bang on the door and the hairy voice that came through.

"All out!"

"Yes," she said, without knowing it.

"You're losing a fortune, Hattie. Shame on a fine, strapping woman like you, black-facing herself up like this when you've hit on something with a fortune in it if you work it properly. You ought to have more regard for the girl. Black-face!"

"What has her—father's regard done for her? It's my black-face has kept her like a lily!"

"Admitting all that you say about me is right. Well, I'm here eating humble pie now. If that little girl doesn't know, bless my heart, I'm willin' she shouldn't ever know. I'll take you out to Greenwich to-morrow and marry you. Then what you've told her all these years is the truth. I've just come back, that's all. We've patched up. It's done every day. Right promoting and a few hundred dollars in that there cream will—"

She laughed. November rain running off a broken spout. Yellow leaves scuttling ahead of wind.

"The picture puzzle is now complete, Morton. Your whole scheme, piece by piece. You're about as subtle as corn bread. Well, my answer to you again is, 'Get out!'"

"All right. All right. But we'll both get out, Hattie. Come, I'm a-goin' to call on you-all up home a little while this evenin'!"

"No. It's late. She's—"

"Come, Hattie, you know I'm a-goin' to see that girl one way or another. If you want me to catch that fruit steamer to-morrow, if I were you I'd let me see her my way. You know I'm not much on raisin' my voice, but if I were you, Hattie, I wouldn't fight me."

"Morton—Morton, listen! If you'll take that fruit steamer without trying to see her—would you? You're on your uppers. I understand. Would a hundred—two hundred—"

"I used to light my cigarette with that much down on my rice swamps—"

"You see, Morton, she's such a little thing. A little thing with big eyes. All her life those eyes have looked right down into me, believing everything I ever told her. About you too, Morton. Good things. Not that I'm ashamed of anything I ever told her. My only wrong was ignorance. And innocence. Innocence of the kind of lesson I was to learn from you."

"Nothin' was ever righted by harping on it, Hattie."

"But I want you to understand—O God, make him understand—she's such a sensitive little thing. And as things stand now—glad I'm her mother. Yes, glad—black-face and all! Why, many's the time I've gone home from the theater, too tired to take off my make-up until I got into my own rocker with my ankles soaking in warm water. They swell so terribly sometimes. Rheumatism, I guess. Well, many a time when I kissed her in her sleep she's opened her eyes on me—black-face and all. Her arms up and around me. I was there underneath the black! She knows that! And that's what she'll always know about me, no matter what you tell her. I'm there—her mother—underneath the black! You hear, Morton! That's why you must let us—live—"

"My proposition is the mighty decent one of a gentleman."

"She's only a little baby, Morton. And just at that age where being like all the other boys and girls is the whole of her little life. It's killing—all her airiness and fads and fancies. Such a proper little young lady. You know, the way they clip and trim them at finishing school. Sweet-sixteen nonsense that she'll outgrow. To-night, Morton, she's at a party. A boy's. Her first. That fine-looking yellow-haired young fellow and his sister that bring her home every afternoon. At their house. Gramercy Park. A fine young fellow—Phi Pi—"

"Looka here, Hattie, are you talking against time?"

"She's home asleep by now. I told her she had to be in bed by eleven. She minds me, Morton. I wouldn't—couldn't—wake her. Morton, Morton, she's yours as much as mine. That's God's law, no matter how much man's law may have let you shirk your responsibility. Don't hurt your own flesh and blood by coming back to us—now. I remember once when you cut your hand it made you ill. Blood! Blood is warm. Red. Sacred stuff. She's your blood, Morton. You let us alone when we needed you. Leave us alone, now that we don't!"

"But you do, Hattie girl. That's just it. You're running things a woman's way. Why, a man with the right promoting ideas—"

There was a fusillade of bangs on the door now, and a shout as if the hair on the voice were rising in anger.

"All out or the doors 'll be locked on yuh! Fine doings!"

She grasped her light wrap from its hook, and her hat with its whirl of dark veil, fitting it down with difficulty over the fizz of wig.

"Come, Morton," she said, suddenly. "I'm ready. You're right, now or never."

"Your face!"

"No time now. Later—at home! She'll know that I'm there—under the black!"

"So do I, Hattie. That's why I—"

"I'm not one of the ready-made heroines you read about. That's not my idea of sacrifice! I'd let my child hang her head of my shame sooner than stand up and marry you to save her from it. Marcia wouldn't want me to! She's got your face—but my character! She'll fight! She'll glory that I had the courage to let you tell her the—truth! Yes, she will," she cried, her voice pleading for the truth of what her words exclaimed. "She'll glory in having saved me— from you! You can come! Now, too, while I have the strength that loathing you can give me. I don't want you skulking about. I don't want you hanging over my head—or hers! You can tell her to-night—but in my presence! Come!"

"Yes, sir," he repeated, doggedly and still more doggedly. "Yes, siree!" Following her, trying to be grim, but his lips too soft to click. "Yes—sir!"

They drove up silently through a lusterless midnight with a threat of rain in it, hitting loosely against each other in a shiver-my-timbers taxicab. Her pallor showing through the brown of her face did something horrid to her.

It was as if the skull of her, set in torment, were looking through a transparent black mask, but, because there were not lips, forced to grin.

And yet, do you know that while she rode with him Hattie's heart was high? So high that when she left him finally, seated in her little lamplit living room, it was he whose unease began to develop.

"I—If she's asleep, Hattie—"

Her head looked so sure. Thrust back and sunk a little between the shoulders.

"If she's asleep, I'll wake her. It's better this way. I'm glad, now. I want her to see me save myself. She would want me to. You banked on mock heroics from me, Morton. You lost."

Marcia was asleep, in her narrow, pretty bed with little bowknots painted on the pale wood. About the room all the tired and happy muss of after-the-party. A white-taffeta dress with a whisper of real lace at the neck, almost stiffishly seated, as if with Marcia's trimness, on a chair. A steam of white tulle on the dressing table. A buttonhole gardenia in a tumbler of water. One long white-kid glove on the table beside the night light. A naked cherub in a high hat, holding a pink umbrella for the lamp shade.

"Dear me! Dear me!" screamed Hattie to herself, fighting to keep her mind on the plane of casual things. "She's lost a glove again. Dear me! Dear me! I hope it's a left one to match up with the right one she saved from the last pair. Dear me!"

She picked up a white film of stocking, turning and exploring with spread fingers in the foot part for holes. There was one! Marcia's big toe had danced right through. "Dear me!"

Marcia sleeping. Very quietly and very deeply. She slept like that. Whitely and straightly and with the covers scarcely raised for the ridge of her slim body.

Sometimes Marcia asleep could frighten Hattie. There was something about her white stilliness. Lilies are too fair and so must live briefly. That thought could clutch so that she would kiss Marcia awake. Kiss her soundly because Marcia's sleep could be so terrifyingly deep.

"Marcia," said Hattie, and stood over her bed. Then again, "Mar-cia!" On more voice than she thought her dry throat could yield her.

There was the merest flip of black on the lacy bosom of Marcia's nightgown, and Hattie leaned down to fleck it. No. It was a pin—a small black-enameled pin edged in pearls. Automatically Hattie knew.

"Pi Phi!"

"Marcia," cried Hattie, and shook her a little. She hated so to waken her. Always had. Especially for school on rainy days. Sometimes didn't. Couldn't. Marcia came up out of sleep so reluctantly. A little dazed. A little secretive. As if a white bull in a dream had galloped off with her like Persephone's.

Only Hattie did not know of Persephone. She only knew that Marcia slept beautifully and almost breathlessly. Sweet and low. It seemed silly, sleeping beautifully. But just the same, Marcia did.

Then Hattie, not faltering, mind you, waited. It was better that Marcia should know. Now, too, while her heart was so high.

Sometimes it took as many as three kisses to awaken Marcia. Hattie bent for the first one, a sound one on the tip of her lip.

"Marcia!" she cried. "Marcy, wake up!" and drew back.

Something had happened! Darkly. A smudge the size of a quarter and the color of Hattie's guaranteed-not-to-fade cheek, lay incredibly on Marcia's whiteness.

Hattie had smudged Marcia! *Hattie Had Smudged Marcia!*

There it lay on her beautiful, helpless whiteness. Hattie's smudge.

* * * * *

It is doubtful, from the way he waited with his soft hat dangling from soft fingers, if Morton had ever really expected anything else. Momentary unease gone, he was quiet and Southern and even indolent about it.

"We'll go to Greenwich first thing in the morning and be married," he said.

"Sh-h-h!" she whispered to his quietness. "Don't wake Marcia."

"Hattie—" he said, and started to touch her.

"Don't!" she sort of cried under her whisper, but not without noting that his hand was ready enough to withdraw. "Please—go—now—"

"To-morrow at the station, then. Eleven. There's a train every hour for Greenwich."

He was all tan to her now, standing there like a blur.

"Yes, Morton, I'll be there. If—please—you'll go now."

"Of course," he said. "Late. Only I—Well, paying the taxi—strapped me—temporarily. A ten spot—old Hat—would help."

She gave him her purse, a tiny leather one with a patent clasp. Somehow her fingers were not flexible enough to open it.

His were.

There were a few hours of darkness left, and she sat them out, exactly as he had left her, on the piano stool, looking at the silence.

Toward morning quite an equinoctial storm swept the city, banging shutters and signs, and a steeple on 122d Street was struck by lightning.

And so it was that Hattie's wedding day came up like thunder.

GUILTY

To the swift hiss of rain down soot-greasy window panes and through a medley of the smells of steam off wet overcoats and a pale stench of fish, a judge turned rather tired Friday-afternoon eyes upon the prisoner at the bar, a smallish man in a decent-enough salt-and-pepper suit and more salt than pepper in his hair and mustache.

"You have heard the charge against you," intoned the judge in the holy and righteous key of justice about to be administered. "Do you plead guilty or not guilty?"

"I—I plead guilty of not having told her facts that would have helped her to struggle against the—the thing—her inheritance."

"You must answer the Court directly. Do you—"

"You see, Your Honor—my little girl—so little—my promise. Yes, yes, I—I plead guilty of keeping her in ignorance of what she should have known, but you see, Your Honor, my little gi—"

"Order! Answer to the point. Do you," began the judge again, "plead guilty or not guilty?" his tongue chiming the repetition into the waiting silence like a clapper into a bell.

The prisoner at the bar thumbed his derby hat after the immemorial dry-fingered fashion of the hunted meek, his mouth like an open wound puckering to close.

"Guilty or not guilty, my man? Out with it."

Actually it was not more than a minute or two before the prisoner found reply, but it was long enough for his tortured eye to flash inward and backward with terrible focus....

* * * * *

On its long cross-town block, Mrs. Plush's boarding house repeated itself no less than thirty-odd times. Every front hall of them smelled like cold boiled potato, and the gilt chair in the parlor like banana. At dinner hour thirty-odd basement dining rooms reverberated, not uncheerfully, to the ironstone clatter of the canary-bird bathtub of succotash, the three stewed prunes, or the redolent boiled potato, and on Saturday mornings, almost to the thirty-odd of them, wasp-waisted, oiled-haired young negro girls in white-cotton stockings and cut-down high shoes enormously and rather horribly run down of heel, tilted pints of water over steep stone stoops and scratched at the trickle with old broom runts.

If Mrs. Plush's house broke rank at all, it did so by praiseworthy omission. In that row of the fly-by-night and the van-by-day, the moving or the express wagon seldom backed up before No. 28, except immediately preceding a wedding or following a funeral. And never, in twenty-two years of respectable tenancy, had the furtive lodger oozed, under darkness, through the Plush front door by night, or a huddle of sidewalk trunks and trappings staged the drab domestic tragedy of the dispossessed.

The Kellers (second-story back) had eaten their satisfied way through fourteen years of the breakfasts of apple sauce or cereal; choice of ham and eggs any style or country sausage and buckwheat cakes.

Jeanette Peopping, born in the back parlor, was married out of the front.

On the night that marked the seventeenth anniversary of the Dangs into the third-floor alcove room there was frozen pudding with hot fudge sauce for dessert, and a red-paper bell ringing silently from the dining-room chandelier.

For the eight years of their placid connubiality Mr. and Mrs. Henry Jett had occupied the second-story front.

Stability, that was the word. Why, Mrs. Plush had dealt with her corner butcher for so long that on crowded Saturday mornings it was her custom to step without challenge into the icy zone of the huge refrigerator, herself pinching and tearing back the cold-storage-bitten wings of fowls, weighing them with a fidelity to the ounce, except for a few extra giblets (Mr. Keller loved them), hers, anyhow, most of the time, for the asking.

Even the nearest drug store, wary of that row of the transient hat-on-the-peg, off-the-peg, would deliver to No. 28 a mustard plaster or a deck of cards and charge without question.

To the Jett Fish Company, "Steamers, Hotels, and Restaurants Supplied—If It Swims We Have It," Mrs. Plush paid her bill quarterly only, then Mr. Jett deducting the sum delicately from his board.

So it may be seen that Mrs. Plush's boarding house offered scanty palate to the dauber in local color.

On each of the three floors was a bathroom, spotlessly clean, with a neat hand-lettered sign over each tin tub:

DO UNTO OTHERS AS YOU WOULD HAVE THEM DO UNTO YOU

PLEASE WASH OUT THE TUB AFTER YOU

Upon the outstanding occasion of the fly in the soup and Mr. Keller's subsequent deathly illness, the regrettable immersion had been directly traceable, not to the kitchen, but to the dining-room ceiling. It was November, a season of heavy dipterous mortality. Besides, Mrs. Peopping had seen it fall.

Nor entered here the dirge of the soggy towel; Mrs. Plush placed fluffy stacks of them outside each door each morning. Nor groggy coffee; Mrs. Plush was famous for hers. Drip coffee, boiled up to an angry sea and half an eggshell dropped in like a fairy barque, to settle it.

The Jetts, with whom we have really to do, drank two cups apiece at breakfast. Mrs. Jett, to the slight aid and abetment of one of her two rolls, stopped right there; Mr. Jett plunging on into choice-of—

The second roll Mrs. Jett usually carried away with her from the table. Along about ten o'clock she was apt to feel faint rather than hungry.

"Gone," she called it. "Feeling a little gone."

Not that there was a suggestion of frailty about Mrs. Jett. Anything but that. On the contrary, in all the eight years in the boarding house, she held the clean record of not a day in bed, and although her history previous to that time showed as many as fifteen hours a day on duty in the little fancy-goods store of her own proprietorship, those years showed her guilty of only two incapacitated days, and then because she ran an embroidery needle under her finger nail and suffered a slight infection.

Yet there was something about Emma Jett—eight years of married life had not dissipated it—that was not eupeptic; something of the sear and yellow leaf of perpetual spinsterhood. She was a wintry little body whose wide marriage band always hung loosely on her finger with an air of not belonging; wore an invariable knitted shawl iced with beads across her round shoulders, and frizzed her graying bangs, which, although fruit of her scalp, had a set-on look. Even the softness to her kind gray eyes was cozy rather than warm.

She could look out tabbily from above a lap of handiwork, but in her boudoir wrapper of gray flannelette scalloped in black she was scrawny, almost rangy, like a horse whose ribs show.

"I can no more imagine those two courting," Mrs. Keller, a proud twin herself and proud mother of twins, remarked one afternoon to a euchre group. "They must have sat company by correspondence. Why, they won't even kiss when he comes home if there's anybody in the room!"

"They kiss, all right," volunteered Mrs. Dang of the bay-window alcove room, "and she waves him good-by every morning clear down the block."

"You can't tell about anybody nowadays," vouchsafed some one, tremendously.

But in the end the consensus of opinion, unanimous to the vote, was: Lovely woman, Mrs. Jett.

Nice couple; so unassuming. The goodness looks out of her face; and so reserved!

But it was this aura of reserve that kept Mrs. Jett, not without a bit of secret heartache about it, as remote from the little world about her as the yolk of an egg is remote from the white. Surrounded, yet no part of those surroundings. No osmosis took place.

Almost daily, in some one or another's room, over Honiton lace or the making of steel-bead chatelaine bags, then so much in vogue, those immediate, plushy-voiced gatherings of the members of the plain gold circle took place. Delicious hours of confidence, confab, and the exchanges of the connubially loquacious.

The supreme *lèse majesté* of the married woman who wears her state of wedlock like a crown of blessed thorns; bleeds ecstatically and swaps afternoon-long intimacies, made nasty by the plush in her voice, with her sisters of the matrimonial dynasty.

Mrs. Jett was also bidden, by her divine right, to those conclaves of the wives, and faithfully she attended, but on the rim, as it were. Bitterly silent she sat to the swap of:

"That's nothing. After Jeanette was born my hair began to fall out just as if I had had typhoid"; or, "Both of mine, I am proud to say, were bottle babies"; and once, as she listened, her heart might have been a persimmon, puckering: "The idea for a woman of forty-five to have her first! It's not fair to the child."

They could not, of course, articulate it, but the fact of the matter was not alone that Mrs. Jett was childless (so was Mrs. Dang, who somehow belonged), it was that they sensed, with all the antennae of their busy little intuitions, the ascetic odor of spinsterhood which clung to Mrs. Jett. She was a little "too nice." Would flush at some of the innuendoes of the *contes intimes*, tales of no luster and dulled by soot, but in spite of an inner shrinkage would loop up her mouth to smile, because not to do so was to linger even more remotely outside the privileged rim of the wedding band.

Evenings, after these gatherings, Mrs. Jett was invariably even a bit gentler than her wont in her greetings to Mr. Jett.

Of course, they kissed upon his arrival home, comment to the contrary notwithstanding, in a taken-for-granted fashion, perhaps, but there was something sweet about their utter unexcitement; and had the afternoon session twisted her heart more than usual, Mrs. Jett was apt to place a second kiss lightly upon the black and ever so slightly white mustache, or lay her cheek momentarily to his, as if to atone by thus yearning over him for the one aching and silent void between them.

But in the main Henry Jett was a contented and happy man.

His wife, whom he had met at a church social and wooed in the front of the embroidery and fancy-goods store, fitted him like the proverbial glove—a suede one. In the eight years since, his fish business had almost doubled, and his expenses, if anything, decreased, because more and more it became pleasanter to join in the evening game of no-stakes euchre down in the front parlor or to remain quietly upstairs, a gas lamp on the table between them, Mr. Jett in a dressing gown of hand-embroidered Persian design and a newspaper which he read from first to last; Mrs. Jett at her tranquil process of fine needlework.

Their room abounded in specimens of it. Centerpieces of rose design. Mounds of cushions stamped in bulldog's head and pipe and appropriately etched in colored floss. A poker hand, upheld by realistic five fingers embroidered to the life, and the cuff button denoted by a blue-glass jewel. Across their bed, making it a dais of incongruous splendor, was flung a great counterpane of embroidered linen, in design as narrative as a battle-surging tapestry and every thread in it woven out of these long, quiet evenings by the lamp side.

He was exceedingly proud of her cunning with a needle, so fine that its stab through the cloth was too slight to be seen, and would lose no occasion to show off the many evidences of her delicate workmanship that were everywhere about the room.

"It's like being able to create a book or a piece of music, Em, to say all that on a piece of cloth with nothing but a needle."

"It's a good thing I am able to create something, Henry," placing her thimbled hand on his shoulder and smiling down. She was slightly the taller.

It was remarkable how quick and how tender his intuitions could be. An innuendo from her, faint as the brush of a wing, and he would immediately cluck with his tongue and throw out quite a bravado of chest.

"You're all right, Em. You suit me."

"And you suit me, Henry," stroking his hand.

This he withdrew. It was apt to smell of fish and he thought that once or twice he had noticed her draw back from it, and, anyway, he was exceedingly delicate about the cling of the rottenly pungent fish odor of his workdays.

Not that he minded personally. He had long ago ceased to have any consciousness of the vapors that poured from the bins and the incoming catches into his little partitioned-off office. But occasionally he noticed that in street cars noses would begin to crinkle around him, and every once in a while, even in a crowded conveyance he would find himself the center of a little oasis of vacant seats which he had created around himself.

Immediately upon his arrival home, although his hands seldom touched the fish, he would wash them in a solution of warm water and carbolic acid, and most of the time he changed his suit before dinner, from a salt-and-pepper to a pepper-and-salt, the only sartorial variety in which he ever indulged.

His wife was invariably touched by this little nicety of his, and sometimes bravely forced his hand to her cheek to prove her lack of repugnance.

Boarding-house lore had it correctly. They were an exceedingly nice couple, the Jetts.

One day in autumn, with the sky the color and heaviness of a Lynnhaven oyster, Mrs. Jett sat quite unusually forward on her chair at one of the afternoon congresses of the wives, convened in Mrs. Peopping's back parlor, Jeanette Peopping, aged four, sweet and blond, whom the Jetts loved to borrow Sunday mornings, while she was still in her little nightdress, playing paper dolls in the background.

Her embroidery hoop, with a large shaded pink rose in the working, had, contrary to her custom, fallen from idle hands, and instead of following the dart of the infinitesimal needle, Mrs. Jett's eyes were burningly upon Mrs. Peopping, following, with almost lip-reading intensity, that worthy lady's somewhat voluptuous mouthings.

She was a large, light person with protuberant blue eyes that looked as if at some time they had been two-thirds choked from their sockets and a characteristic of opening every sentence with her mouth shaped to an explosive O, which she filled with as much breath as it would hold.

It had been a long tale of obstetrical fact and fancy, told plushily, of course, against the dangerous little ears of Jeanette, and at its conclusion Mrs. Peopping's steel-bead bag, half finished, lay in a huddle at her feet, her pink and flabby face turned reminiscently toward the fire.

"—and for three days six doctors gave me up. Why, I didn't see Jeanette until the fourteenth day, when most women are up and out. The crisis, you know. My night nurse, an awful sweet girl—I send her a Christmas present to this day—said if I had been six years younger it wouldn't have gone so hard with me. I always say if the men knew what we women go through—Maybe if some of them had to endure the real pain themselves they would have something to do besides walk up and down the hall and turn pale at the smell of ether coming through the keyhole. Ah me! I've been a great sufferer in my day."

"Thu, thu, thu," and, "I could tell tales," and, "I've been through my share"— from various points of vantage around the speaker.

It was then that Mrs. Jett sat forward on the edge of the straight chair, and put her question.

There was a pause after it had fallen into the silence, as if an intruder had poked her head in through the door, and it brought only the most negligible answer from Mrs. Peopping.

"Forty-three."

Almost immediately Mrs. Dang caught at the pause for a case in point that had been trembling on her lips all during Mrs. Peopping's recital.

"A doctor once told a second cousin of my sister-in-law's—" and so on *ad infinitum, ad lib.,* and *ad nauseaum.*

That night Mrs. Jett did an unprecedented thing. She crept into the crevice of her husband's arm from behind as he stood in his waistcoat, washing his hands in the carbolic solution at the bowl and washstand. He turned, surprised, unconsciously placing himself between her and the reeky water.

"Henry," she said, rubbing up against the alpaca back to his vest like an ingratiating Maltese tabby, "Hen-ery."

"In a minute, Em," he said, rather puzzled and wishing she would wait.

Suddenly, swinging herself back from him by his waistcoat lapel, easily, because of his tenseness to keep her clear of the bowl of water, she directed her eyes straight into his.

"Hen-ery—Hen-ery," each pronouncement of his name surging higher in her throat.

"Why, Em?"

"Hen-ery, I haven't words sweet enough to tell you."

"Em, tell what?" And stopped. He could see suddenly that her eyes were full of new pins of light and his lightening intuition performed a miracle of understanding.

"Emmy!" he cried, jerking her so that her breath jumped, and at the sudden drench of tears down her face sat her down, supporting her roundish back with his wet hands, although he himself felt weak.

"I—can't say—what I feel, Henry—only—God is good and—I'm not afraid."

He held her to his shoulder and let her tears rain down into his watch pocket, so shaken that he found himself mouthing silent words.

"God is good, Henry, isn't He?"

"Yes, Emmy, yes. Oh, my Emmy!"

"It must have been our prayers, Henry."

"Well," sheepishly, "not exactly mine, Emmy; you're the saint of this family. But I—I've wished."

"Henry. I'm so happy—Mrs. Peopping had Jeanette at forty-three. Three years older than me. I'm not afraid."

It was then he looked down at her graying head there, prone against his chest, and a dart of fear smote him.

"Emmy," he cried, dragging her tear-happy face up to his, "if you're afraid— not for anything in the world! You're *first*, Em."

She looked at him with her eyes two lamps.

"Afraid? That's the beautiful *part*, Henry. I'm not. Only happy. Why afraid, Henry—if others dare it at—forty-three—You mean because it was her second?"

He faced her with a scorch of embarrassment in his face.

"You—We—Well, we're not spring chickens any more, Em. If you are sure it's not too—"

She hugged him, laughing her tears.

"I'm all right, Henry—we've been too happy not to—to—perpetuate—it."

This time he did not answer. His cheek was against the crochet of her yoke and she could hear his sobs with her heart.

* * * * *

Miraculously, like an amoeba reaching out to inclose unto itself, the circle opened with a gasp of astonishment that filled Mrs. Peopping's O to its final stretch and took unto its innermost Emma Jett.

Nor did she wear her initiation lightly. There was a new tint out in her long cheeks, and now her chair, a rocker, was but one removed from Mrs. Peopping's.

Oh, the long, sweet afternoons over garments that made needlework sublime. No longer the padded rose on the centerpiece or the futile doily, but absurd little dresses with sleeves that she measured to the length of her hand, and yokes cut out to the pattern of a playing card, and all fretted over with feather-stitching that was frailer than maidenhair fern and must have cost many an eye-ache, which, because of its source, was easy to bear.

And there happened to Mrs. Jett that queer juvenescence that sometimes comes to men and women in middle life. She who had enjoyed no particular youth (her father had died in a ferryboat crash two weeks before her birth, and her mother three years after) came suddenly to acquire comeliness which her youth had never boasted.

The round-shouldered, long-cheeked girl had matured gingerly to rather sparse womanhood that now at forty relented back to a fulsome thirty.

Perhaps it was the tint of light out in her face, perhaps the splendor of the vision; but at any rate, in those precious months to come, Mrs. Jett came to look herself as she should have looked ten years back.

They were timid and really very beautiful together, she and Henry Jett. He came to regard her as a vase of porcelain, and, in his ignorance, regarded the doctor's mandates harsh; would not permit her to walk, but ordered a hansom cab every day from three to four, Mrs. Jett alternating punctiliously with each of the boarding-house ladies for driving companion.

Every noon, for her delectation at luncheon, he sent a boy from the store with a carton of her special favorites—Blue Point oysters. She suddenly liked them small because, as she put it, they went down easier, and he thought that charming. Lynnhavens for mortals of tougher growth.

Long evenings they spent at names, exercising their pre-determination as to sex. "Ann" was her choice, and he was all for canceling his preference for "Elizabeth," until one morning she awakened to the white light of inspiration.

"I have it! Why not Ann Elizabeth?"

"Great!" And whistled so through his shaving that his mouth was rayed with a dark sunburst of beard where the razor had not found surface.

They talked of housekeeping, reluctantly, it is true, because Mrs. Plush herself was fitting up, of hard-to-spare evenings, a basinette of pink and white. They even talked of schools.

Then came the inevitable time when Mrs. Jett lost interest. Quite out of a clear sky even the Blue Points were taboo, and instead of joining this or that card or sewing circle, there were long afternoons of stitching away alone, sometimes the smile out on her face, sometimes not.

"Em, is it all right with you?" Henry asked her once or twice, anxiously.

"Of course it is! If I weren't this way—now—it wouldn't be natural. You don't understand."

He didn't, so could only be vaguely and futilely sorry.

Then one day something quite horrible, in a small way, happened to Mrs. Jett. Sitting sewing, suddenly it seemed to her that through the very fluid of her eyeballs, as it were, floated a school of fish. Small ones—young smelts, perhaps—with oval lips, fillips to their tails, and sides that glisted.

She laid down her bit of linen lawn, fingers to her lids as if to squeeze out their tiredness. She was trembling from the unpleasantness, and for a frightened moment could not swallow. Then she rose, shook out her skirts, and to be rid of the moment carried her sewing up to Mrs. Dang's, where a euchre game was in session, and by a few adroit questions in between deals gained the reassurance that a nervous state in her "condition" was highly normal.

She felt easier, but there was the same horrid recurrence three times that week. Once during an evening of lotto down in the front parlor she pushed back from the table suddenly, hand flashing up to her throat.

"Em!" said Mr. Jett, who was calling the numbers.

"It's nothing," she faltered, and then, regaining herself more fully, "nothing," she repeated, the roundness out in her voice this time.

The women exchanged knowing glances.

"She's all right," said Mrs. Peopping, omnipotently. "Those things pass."

Going upstairs that evening, alone in the hallway, they flung an arm each across the other's shoulder, crowding playfully up the narrow flight.

"Emmy," he said, "poor Em, everything will be all right."

She restrained an impulse to cry. "Poor nothing," she said.

But neither the next evening, which was Friday, nor for Fridays thereafter, would she venture down for fish dinner, dining cozily up in her room off milk toast and a fluffy meringue dessert prepared especially by Mrs. Plush. It was floating-island night downstairs.

Henry puzzled a bit over the Fridays. It was his heaviest day at the business, and it was upsetting to come home tired and feel her place beside him at the basement dinner table vacant.

But the women's nods were more knowing than ever, the reassuring insinuations more and more delicate.

But one night, out of one of those stilly cisterns of darkness that between two and four are deepest with sleep, Henry was awakened on the crest of such a blow and yell that he swam up to consciousness in a ready-made armor of high-napped gooseflesh.

A regrettable thing had happened. Awakened, too, on the high tide of what must have been a disturbing dream, Mrs. Jett flung out her arm as if to ward off something. That arm encountered Henry, snoring lightly in his sleep at her side. But, unfortunately, to that frightened fling of her arm Henry did not translate himself to her as Henry.

That was a fish lying there beside her! A man-sized fish with its mouth jerked open to the shape of a gasp and the fillip still through its enormous body, as if its flanks were uncomfortably dry. A fish!

With a shriek that tore a jagged rent through the darkness Mrs. Jett began pounding at the slippery flanks, her hands sliding off its shininess.

"Out! Out! Henry, where are you? Help me! O God, don't let him get me. Take him away, Henry! Where are you? My hands—slippery! Where are you—"

Stunned, feeling for her in the darkness, he wanted to take her shuddering form into his arms and waken her out of this horror, but with each groping move of his her hurtling shrieks came faster, and finally, dragging the bedclothing with her, she was down on the floor at the bedside, blobbering. That is the only word for it—blobbering.

He found a light, and by this time there were already other lights flashing up in the startled household. When he saw her there in the ague of a huddle on the floor beside the bed, a cold sweat broke out over him so that he could almost feel each little explosion from the pores.

"Why, Emmy—Emmy—my Emmy—my Emmy—"

She saw him now and knew him, and tried in her poor and already burningly ashamed way to force her chattering jaws together.

"Hen-ery—dream—bad—fish—Hen-ery—"

He drew her up to the side of the bed, covering her shivering knees as she sat there, and throwing a blanket across her shoulders. Fortunately he was aware that the soothing note in his voice helped, and so he sat down beside her, stroking her hand, stroking, almost as if to hypnotize her into quiet.

"Henry," she said, closing her fingers into his wrists, "I must have dreamed— a horrible dream. Get back to bed, dear. I—I don't know what ails me, waking up like that. That—fish! O God! Henry, hold me, hold me."

He did, lulling her with a thousand repetitions of his limited store of endearments, and he could feel the jerk of sobs in her breathing subside and she seemed almost to doze, sitting there with her far hand across her body and up against his cheek.

Then came knocks at the door, and hurried explanations through the slit that he opened, and Mrs. Peopping's eye close to the crack.

"Everything is all right.... Just a little bad dream the missus had.... All right now.... To be expected, of course.... No, nothing anyone can do.... Good night. Sorry.... No, thank you. Everything is all right."

The remainder of the night the Jetts kept a small light burning, after a while Henry dropping off into exhausted and heavy sleep. For hours Mrs. Jett lay staring at the small bud of light, no larger than a human eye. It seemed to stare back at her, warning, Now don't you go dropping off to sleep and misbehave again.

And holding herself tense against a growing drowsiness, she didn't—for fear—

* * * * *

The morning broke clear, and for Mrs. Jett full of small reassurances. It was good to hear the clatter of milk deliveries, and the first bar of sunshine came in through the hand-embroidered window curtains like a smile, and she could smile back. Later she ventured down shamefacedly for the two cups of coffee, which she drank bravely, facing the inevitable potpourri of comment from this one and that one.

"That was a fine scare you gave us last night, Mrs. Jett."

"I woke up stiff with fright. Didn't I, Will? Gracious! That first yell was a curdler!"

"Just before Jeanette was born I used to have bad dreams, too, but nothing like that. My!"

"My mother had a friend whose sister-in-law walked in her sleep right out of a third-story window and was dashed to—"

"Shh-h-h!"

"It's natural, Mrs. Jett. Don't you worry."

She really tried not to, and after some subsequent and private reassurance from Mrs. Peopping and Mrs. Keller, went for her hansom ride with a pleasant anticipation of the Park in red leaf, Mrs. Plush, in a brocade cape with ball fringe, sitting erect beside her.

One day, in the presence of Mrs. Peopping, Mrs. Jett jumped to her feet with a violent shaking of her right hand, as if to dash off something that had crawled across its back.

"Ugh!" she cried. "It flopped right on my hand. A minnow! Ugh!"

"A what?" cried Mrs. Peopping, jumping to her feet and her flesh seeming to crawl up.

"A minnow. I mean a bug—a June bug. It was a bug, Mrs. Peopping."

There ensued a mock search for the thing, the two women, on all-fours, peering beneath the chairs. In that position they met levelly, eye to eye. Then without more ado rose, brushing their knees and reseating themselves.

"Maybe if you would read books you would feel better," said Mrs. Peopping, scooping up a needleful of steel beads. "I know a woman who made it her business to read all the poetry books she could lay hands on, and went to all the bandstand concerts in the Park the whole time, and now her daughter sings in the choir out in Saginaw, Michigan."

"I know some believe in that," said Mrs. Jett, trying to force a smile through her pallor. "I must try it."

But the infinitesimal stitching kept her so busy.

* * * * *

It was inevitable, though, that in time Henry should begin to shoulder more than a normal share of unease.

One evening she leaned across the little lamplit table between them as he sat reading in the Persian-design dressing gown and said, as rapidly as her lips could form the dreadful repetition, "The fish, the fish, the fish, the fish." And then, almost impudently for her, disclaimed having said it.

He urged her to visit her doctor and she would not, and so, secretly, he did, and came away better satisfied, and with directions for keeping her diverted, which punctiliously he tried to observe.

He began by committing sly acts of discretion on his own accord. Was careful not to handle the fish. Changed his suit now before coming home, behind a screen in his office, and, feeling foolish, went out and purchased a bottle of violet eau de Cologne, which he rubbed into his palms and for some inexplicable reason on his half-bald spot.

Of course that was futile, because the indescribably and faintly rotten smell of the sea came through, none the less, and to Henry he was himself heinous with scent.

One Sunday morning, as was his wont, Mr. Jett climbed into his dressing gown and padded downstairs for the loan of little Jeanette Peopping, with whom he returned, the delicious nub of her goldilocks head showing just above the blanket which enveloped her, eyes and all.

He deposited her in bed beside Mrs. Jett, the little pink feet peeping out from her nightdress and her baby teeth showing in a smile that Mr. Jett loved to pinch together with thumb and forefinger.

"Cover her up quick, Em, it's chilly this morning."

Quite without precedent, Jeanette puckered up to cry, holding herself rigidly to Mr. Jett's dressing gown.

"Why, Jeanette baby, don't you want to go to Aunty Em?"

"No! No! No!" Trying to ingratiate herself back into Mr. Jett's arms.

"Baby, you'll take cold. Come under covers with Aunty Em?"

"No! No! No! Take me back."

"Oh, Jeanette, that isn't nice! What ails the child? She's always so eager to come to me. Shame on Jeanette! Come, baby, to Aunty Em?"

"No! No! No! My mamma says you're crazy. Take me back—take me."

For a frozen moment Henry regarded his wife above the glittering fluff of little-girl curls. It seemed to him he could almost see her face become smaller, like a bit of ice under sun.

"Naughty little Jeanette," he said, shouldering her and carrying her down the stairs; "naughty little girl."

When he returned his wife was sitting locked in the attitude in which he had left her.

"Henry!" she whispered, reaching out and closing her hand over his so that the nails bit in. "Not that, Henry! Tell me not that!"

"Why, Em," he said, sitting down and trembling, "I'm surprised at you, listening to baby talk! Why, Em, I'm surprised at you!"

She leaned over, shaking him by the shoulder.

"I know. They're saying it about me. I'm not that, Henry. I swear I'm not that! Always protect me against their saying that, Henry. Not crazy—not that! It's natural for me to feel queer at times—now. Every woman in this house who says—that—about me has had her nervous feelings. It's not quite so easy for me, as if I were a bit younger. That's all. The doctor said that. But nothing to worry about. Mrs. Peopping had Jeanette—Oh, Henry promise me you'll always protect me against their saying that! I'm not that—I swear to you, Henry—not that!"

"I know you're not, Emmy. It's too horrible and too ridiculous to talk about. Pshaw—pshaw!"

"You do know I'm not, don't you? Tell me again you do know."

"I do. Do."

"And you'll always protect me against anyone saying it? They'll believe you, Henry, not me. Promise me to protect me against them, Henry. Promise to protect me against our little Ann Elizabeth ever thinking that of—of her mother."

"Why, Emmy!" he said. "Why, Emmy! I just promise a thousand times—" and could not go on, working his mouth rather foolishly as if he had not teeth and were rubbing empty gums together.

But through her hot gaze of tears she saw and understood and, satisfied, rubbed her cheek against his arm.

The rest is cataclysmic.

Returning home one evening in a nice glow from a January out-of-doors, his mustache glistening with little frozen drops and his hands (he never wore gloves) unbending of cold, Mrs. Jett rose at her husband's entrance from her low chair beside the lamp.

"Well, well!" he said, exhaling heartily, the scent of violet denying the pungency of fish and the pungency of fish denying the scent of violet. "How's the busy bee this evening?"

For answer Mrs. Jett met him with the crescendo yell of a gale sweeping around a chimney.

"Ya-a-ah! Keep out—you! Fish! Fish!" she cried, springing toward him; and in the struggle that ensued the tubing wrenched off the gas lamp and plunged them into darkness. "Fish! I'll fix you! Ya-a-ah!"

"Emmy! For God's sake, it's Henry! Em!"

"Ya-a-ah! I'll fix you! Fish! Fish!"

* * * * *

Two days later Ann Elizabeth was born, beautiful, but premature by two weeks.

Emma Jett died holding her tight against her newly rich breasts, for a few of the most precious and most fleeting moments of her life.

All her absurd fears washed away, her free hand could lie without spasm in Henry's, and it was as if she found in her last words a secret euphony that delighted her.

"Ann-Elizabeth. Sweet-beautiful. Ann-Elizabeth. Sweet-beautiful."

Later in his bewildered and almost ludicrous widowerhood tears would sometimes galumph down on his daughter's face as Henry rocked her of evenings and Sunday mornings.

"Sweet-beautiful," came so absurdly from under his swiftly graying mustache, but often, when sure he was quite alone, he would say it over and over again.

"Sweet-beautiful. Ann-Elizabeth. Sweet-beautiful. Ann-Elizabeth."

* * * * *

Of course the years puttied in and healed and softened, until for Henry almost a Turner haze hung between him and some of the stark facts of Emma Jett's death, turping out horror, which is always the first to fade from memory, and leaving a dear sepia outline of the woman who had been his.

At seventeen, Ann Elizabeth was the sun, the sky, the west wind, and the shimmer of spring—all gone into the making of her a rosebud off the stock of his being.

His way of putting it was, "You're my all, Annie, closer to me than I am to myself."

She hated the voweling of her name, and because she was so nimble with youth could dance away from these moods of his rather than plumb them.

"I won't be 'Annie.' Please, daddy, I'm your Ann Elizabeth."

"Ann Elizabeth, then. My Ann Elizabeth," an inner rhythm in him echoing: Sweet-Beautiful. Sweet-Beautiful.

There was actually something of the lark about her. She awoke with a song, sometimes kneeling up in bed, with her pretty brown hair tousling down over her shoulders and chirruping softly to herself into the little bird's-eye-maple dressing-table mirror, before she flung her feet over the side of the bed.

And then, innate little housekeeper that she was, it was to the preparing of breakfast with a song, her early morning full of antics. Tiptoeing in to awaken her father to the tickle of a broom straw. Spreading his breakfast piping hot, and then concealing herself behind a screen, that he might marvel at the magic of it. And once she put salt in his coffee, a fresh cup concealed behind the toast rack, and knee to knee they rocked in merriment at his grimace.

She loved thus to tease him, probably because he was so stolid that each new adventure came to him with something of a shock. He was forever being taken unawares, as if he could never become entirely accustomed to the wonder of her, and that delighted her. Even the obviousness of his slippers stuffed out with carrots could catch him napping. To her dance of glee behind him, he kept poking and poking to get into them, only the peck of her kiss upon his neck finally initiating him into the absurdity.

There was a little apartment of five rooms, twenty minutes removed by Subway from the fish store; her bedroom, all pink and yellow maple; his; a kitchen, parlor, and dining room worked out happily in white-muslin curtains, spindle-legged parlor chairs, Henry's newfangled chifferobe and bed with a fine depth of mattress, and a kitchen with eight shining pots above the sink and a border of geese, cut out to the snip of Ann's own scissors, waddling across the wall.

It was two and a half years since Mrs. Plush had died, and the boarders, as if spilled from an ark on rough seas, had struck out for diverse shores. The marvel to them now was that they had delayed so long.

"A home of our own, Ann. Pretty sweet, isn't it?"

"Oh, daddy, it is!"

"You mustn't overdo, though, baby. Sometimes we're not so strong as we think we are. A little hired girl would be best." The fish business had more than held its own.

"But I love doing it alone, dad. It—it's the next best thing to a home of—my own."

He looked startled into her dreaming eyes.

"Your own? Why, Annie, isn't this—your own?"

She laid fingers against his eyes so that he could not see the pinkiness of her.

"You know what I mean, daddy—my—very—own."

At that timid phrasing of hers Henry felt that his heart was actually strangling, as if some one were holding it back on its systolic swing, like a caught pendulum.

"Why, Annie," he said, "I never thought—"

But inevitably and of course it had happened.

The young man's name was Willis—Fred E. Willis—already credit man in a large wholesale grocery firm and two feet well on the road to advancement.

A square-faced, clean-faced fellow, with a clean love of life and of Ann Elizabeth in his heart.

Henry liked him.

Ann Elizabeth loved him.

And yet, what must have been a long-smoldering flame of fear shot up through the very core of Henry's being, excoriating.

"Why, Ann Elizabeth," he kept repeating, in his slow and always inarticulate manner, "I—You—Mine—I just never thought."

She wound the softest of arms about his neck.

"I know, daddy-darlums, and I'll never leave you. Never. Fred has promised we will always be together. We'll live right here with you, or you with us."

"Annie," he cried, "you mustn't ever—marry. I mean, leave daddy—that way—anyway. You hear me? You're daddy's own. Just his by himself. Nobody is good enough for my girl."

"But, daddy," clouding up for tears, "I thought you liked Fred so much!"

"I do, but it's you I'm talking about. Nobody can have you."

"But I love him, daddy. This is terrible. I love him."

"Oh, Ann, Ann! daddy hasn't done right, perhaps, but he meant well. There are *reasons* why he wants to keep his little girl with him always—alone—his."

"But, daddy dear, I promise you we'll never let you be lonely. Why, I couldn't stand leaving you any more than you could—"

"Not those reasons alone, Ann."

"Then what?"

"You're so young," he tried to procrastinate.

"I'll be eighteen. A woman."

All his faculties were cornered.

"You're—so—Oh, I don't know—I—"

"You haven't any reasons, dad, except dear silly ones. You can't keep me a little girl all the time, dear. I love Fred. It's all planned. Don't ruin my life, daddy—don't ruin my life."

She was lovely in her tears and surprisingly resolute in her mind, and he was more helpless than ever with her.

"Ann—you're not strong."

"Strong!" she cried, flinging back her curls and out her chest. "That is a fine excuse. I'm stronger than most. All youngsters have measles and scarlet fever and Fred says his sister Lucile out in Des Moines had St. Vitus' dance when she was eleven, just like I did. I'm stronger than you are, dad. I didn't get the flu and you did."

"You're nervous, Annie. That's why I want always to keep you at home—quiet—with me."

She sat back, her pretty eyes troubled-up lakes.

"You mean the dreams and the scared feeling, once in a while, that I can't swallow. That's nothing. I know now why I was so frightened in my sleep the other night. I told Fred, and he said it was the peach sundae on top of the crazy old movie we saw that evening. Why, Jeanette Peopping had to take a rest cure the year before she was married. Girls are always more nervous than fellows. Daddy—you—you frighten me when you look at me like that! I don't know what you mean! What-do-you-mean?"

He was helpless and at bay and took her in his arms and kissed her hair.

"I guess your old daddy is a jealous pig and can't bear to share his girl with anyone. Can't bear to—to give her up."

"You won't be giving up, daddums. I couldn't stand that, either. It will be three of us then. You'll see. Look up and smile at your Ann Elizabeth. Smile, now, smile."

And of course he did.

It was typical of her that she should be the busiest of brides-to-be, her complete little trousseau, every piece down to the dishcloths, monogrammed by her—A.E.W.

Skillful with her needle and thrifty in her purchases, the outfit when completed might have represented twice the outlay that Henry expended on it. Then there were "showers,"—linen, stocking, and even a tin one; gifts from her girl friends—cup, face, bath and guest towels; all the tremendous trifles and addenda that go to gladden the chattel-loving heart of a woman. A little secret society of her erstwhile school friends presented her with a luncheon set; the Keller twins with a silver gravy boat; and Jeanette Peopping Truman, who occupied an apartment in the same building, spent as many as three afternoons a week with her, helping to piece out a really lovely tulip-design quilt of pink and white sateen.

"Jeanette," said Ann Elizabeth, one afternoon as the two of them sat in a frothy litter of the pink and white scraps, "how did you feel that time when you had the nerv—the breakdown?"

Jeanette, pretty after a high-cheek-boned fashion and her still bright hair worn coronet fashion about her head, bit off a thread with sharp white teeth, only too eager to reminisce her ills.

"I was just about gone, that's what I was. Let anybody so much as look at me twice and, pop! I'd want to cry about it."

"And?"

"For six weeks I didn't even have enough interest to ask after Truman, who was courting me then. Oh, it was no fun, I can tell you, that nervous breakdown of mine!"

"What—else?"

"Isn't that enough?"

"Did it—was it—was it ever hard to swallow, Jeanette?"

"To swallow?"

"Yes. I mean—did you ever dream or—think—or feel so frightened you couldn't swallow?"

"I felt lots of ways, but that wasn't one of them. Swallow! Who ever heard of not swallowing?"

"But didn't you ever dream, Jeanette—terrible things—such terrible things— and get to thinking and couldn't stop yourself? Silly, ghostly—things."

Jeanette put down her sewing.

"Ann, are you quizzing me about—your mother?"

"My mother? Why my mother? Jeanette, what do you mean? Why do you ask me a thing like that? What has my mother got to do with it? Jeanette!"

Conscious that she had erred, Jeanette veered carefully back.

"Why, nothing, only I remember mamma telling me when I was just a kiddie how your mamma used to—to imagine all sorts of things just to pass the time away while she embroidered the loveliest pieces. You're like her, mamma used to say—a handy little body. Poor mamma, to think she had to be taken before Truman, junior, was born! Ah me!"

That evening, before Fred came for his two hours with her in the little parlor, Ann, rid of her checked apron and her crisp pink frock saved from the grease of frying sparks, flew in from a ring at the doorbell with a good-sized special-delivery box from a silversmith, untying it with eager, fumbling fingers, her father laying aside his newspaper to venture three guesses as to its contents.

"Another one of those syrup pitchers."

"Oh dear!"—plucking the twine—"I hope not!"

"Some more nut picks."

"Daddy, stop calamity howling. Here's the card. Des Moines, Iowa. 'From Lucile Willis, with love to her new sister.' Isn't that the sweetest! It's something with a pearl handle."

"I know. Another one of those pie-spade things."

"Wrong! Wrong! It's two pieces. Oh!"

It was a fish set of silver and mother-of-pearl. A large-bowled spoon and a sort of Neptune's fork, set up in a white-sateen bed.

"Say now, that *is* neat," said Henry, appraising each piece with a show of critical appreciation not really his. All this spread of the gewgaws of approaching nuptials seemed meaningless to him; bored him. Butter knives. Berry spoons. An embarrassment of nut picks and silver pitchers. A sliver of silver paper cutter with a hilt and a dog's-head handle. And now, for Fred's delectation this evening, the newly added fish set, so appropriately inscribed from his sister.

Tilting it against the lamp in the place of honor, Ann Elizabeth turned away suddenly, looking up at her father in a sudden dumb panic of which he knew nothing, her two hands at her fair, bare throat. It was so hard again to swallow. Impossible.

But finally, as was always the case, she did swallow, with a great surge of relief. A little later, seated on her father's knee and plucking at his tie in a futile fashion that he loved, she asked him:

"Daddy—about mother—"

They seldom talked of her, but always during these rare moments a beautiful mood shaped itself between them. It was as if the mere breath of his daughter's sweetly lipped use of "mother" swayed the bitter-sweet memory of the woman he carried so faithfully in the cradle of his heart.

"Yes, baby—about mother?"

"Daddy"—still fingering at the tie—"was mother—was everything all right with her up—to the very—end? I mean—no nerv—no pain? Just all of a sudden the end—quietly. Or have you told me that just to—spare me?"

She could feel him stiffen, but when his voice came it was even.

"Why, Ann, what a—question! Haven't I told you so often how mother just peacefully passed on, holding a little pink you."

Sweet-Beautiful—his heart was tolling through a sense of panic—Sweet-Beautiful.

"I know, daddy, but before—wasn't there any nerv—any sickness?"

"No," he said, rather harshly for him. "No. No. What put such ideas into your head?"

You see, he was shielding Emma way back there, and a typhoon of her words was raging through his head:

"Oh, Henry, protect me against anyone ever saying—that. Promise me."

And now, with no sense of his terrible ruthlessness, he was protecting her with her own daughter.

"Then, daddy, just one more thing," and her underlip caught while she waited for answer. "There is no other reason except your own dear silly one of loneliness—why you keep wanting me to put off my marriage?"

"No, baby," he said, finally, his words with no more depth than if his body were a hollow gourd. "What else could there be?"

Immediately, and with all the resilience of youth, she was her happy self again, kissing him through his mustache and on his now frankly bald head, which gave off the incongruous odor of violet eau de Cologne.

"Old dude daddy!" she cried, and wanted to kiss his hands, which he held suddenly very still and far from her reach.

Then the bell rang again and Fred Willis arrived. All the evening, long after Henry lay on his deep-mattressed bed, staring, the little apartment trilled to her laughter and the basso of Fred's.

* * * * *

A few weeks later there occurred a strike of the delivery men and truck drivers of the city, and Henry, especially hard hit because of the perishable nature of his product, worked early and late, oftentimes loading the wagons himself and riding alongside of the precariously driving "scab."

Frequently he was as much as an hour or two late to dinner, and upon one or two occasions had tiptoed out of the house before the usual hour when Ann opened her eyes to the consciousness of his breakfast to be prepared.

They were trying days, the scheme of his universe broken into, and Henry thrived on routine.

The third week of the strike there were street riots, some of them directly in front of the fish store, and Henry came home after a day of the unaccustomed labor of loading and unloading hampers of fish, really quite shaken.

When he arrived Ann Elizabeth was cutting around the scalloped edge of a doily with embroidery scissors, the litter of cut glass and silver things out on the table and throwing up quite a brilliance under the electric lamp, and from the kitchen the slow sizzle of waiting chops.

"Whew!" he said, as he entered, both from the whiff he emanated as he shook out of his overcoat, and from a great sense of his weariness. Loading the hampers, you understand. "Whew!"

Ann Elizabeth started violently, first at the whiff which preceded him and at his approach into the room; then sat forward, her hand closing into the arm of the chair, body thrust forward and her eyes widening like two flowers opening.

Then she rose slowly and slyly, and edged behind the table, her two hands up about her throat.

"Don't you come in here," she said, lowly and evenly. "I know you, but I'm not afraid. I'm only afraid of you at night, but not by light. You let me swallow, you hear! Get out! Get out!"

Rooted, Henry stood.

"Why, Annie!" he said in the soothing voice from out of his long ago, "Annie—it's daddy!"

"No, you don't," she cried, springing back as he took the step forward. "My daddy'll kill you if he finds you here. He'll slit you up from your tail right up to your gill. He knows how. I'm going to tell him and Fred on you. You won't let me swallow. You're slippery. I can't stand it. Don't you come near me! Don't!"

"Annie!" he cried. "Good God! Annie, it's daddy who loves you!" Poor Henry, her voice was still under a whisper and in his agony he committed the error of rushing at her. "Annie, it's daddy! See, your own dear daddy!"

But she was too quick. Her head thrown back so that the neck muscles strained out like an outraged deer's cornered in the hunt and her eyes rolled up, Ann felt for and grasped the paper knife off the trinket-littered table.

"Don't you touch me—slit you up from tail to your gills."

"Annie, it's daddy! Papa! For God's sake look at daddy—Ann! God!" And caught her wrist in the very act of its plumb-line rush for his heart.

He was sweating in his struggle with her, and most of all her strength appalled him, she was so little for her terrible unaccountable power.

"Don't touch me! You can't! You haven't any arms! Horrible gills!"

She was talking as she struggled, still under the hoarse and frantic whisper, but her breath coming in long soughs. "Slit-you-up-from-tail. Slit—you—up—from—tail—to—gills."

"Annie! Annie!" still obsessed by his anguished desire to reassure her with the normality of his touch. "See, Annie, it's daddy. Ann Elizabeth's daddy." With a flash her arm and the glint of the paper cutter eluded him again and again, but finally he caught her by the waist, struggling, in his dreadful mistake, to calm her down into the chair again.

"Now I've got you, darling. Now—sit—down—"

"No, you haven't," she said, a sort of wild joy coming out in her whisper, and cunningly twisting the upper half of her body back from his, the hand still held high. "You'll never get me—you fish!"

And plunged with her high hand in a straight line down into her throat.

It was only when the coroner withdrew the sliver of paper knife from its whiteness, that, coagulated, the dead and waiting blood began to ooze.

* * * * *

"Do you," intoned the judge for the third and slightly more impatient time, "plead guilty or not guilty to the charge of murder against you?"

This time the lips of the prisoner's wound of a mouth moved stiffly together:

"Guilty."

ROULETTE

I

Snow in the village of Vodna can have the quality of hot white plush of enormous nap, so dryly thick it packs into the angles where fences cross, sealing up the windward sides of houses, rippling in great seas across open places, flaming in brilliancy against the boles of ever so occasional trees, and tucking in the houses up to the sills and down over the eaves.

Out in the wide places it is like a smile on a dead face, this snow hush, grateful that peace can be so utter. It is the silence of a broody God, and out of that frozen pause, in a house tucked up to the sills and down to the eaves, Sara Turkletaub was prematurely taken with the pangs of childbirth, and in the thin dawn, without even benefit of midwife, twin sons were born.

Sturdy sons, with something even in their first crescendo wails that bespoke the good heritage of a father's love-of-life and a mother's life-of-love.

No Sicilian sunrise was ever more glossy with the patina of hope than the iced one that crept in for a look at the wide-faced, high-cheek-boned beauty of Sara Turkletaub as she lay with her sons to the miracle of her full breasts, her hair still rumpled with the agony of deliverance. So sweetly moist her eyes that Mosher Turkletaub, his own brow damp from sweat of her writhings, was full of heartbeat, even to his temples.

Long before moontime, as if by magic of the brittle air, the tidings had spread through the village, and that night, until the hand-hewn rafters rang, the house of Turkletaub heralded with twofold and world-old fervor the advent of the man-child. And through it all—the steaming warmth, the laughter through bushy beards, the ministering of women wise and foolish with the memory of their own pangs, the shouts of vodka-stirred men, sheepish that they, too, were part custodians of the miracle of life—through it all Sara Turkletaub lay back against her coarse bed, so rich—so rich that the coves of her arms trembled each of its burden and held tighter for fear somehow God might repent of his prodigality.

That year the soil came out from under the snow rich and malmy to the plow, and Mosher started heavy with his peddler's pack and returned light. It was no trick now for Sara to tie her sons to an iron ring in the door jamb and, her strong legs straining and her sweat willing, undertake household chores of water lugging, furniture heaving, marketing with baskets that strained her arms from the sockets as she carted them from the open square to their house on the outskirts, her massive silhouette moving as solemnly as a caravan against the sky line.

Rich months these were and easy to bear because they were backed by a dream that each day, however relentless in its toil, brought closer to reality.

"America!"

The long evenings full of the smell of tallow; maps that curled under the fingers; the well-thumbed letters from Aaron Turkletaub, older brother to Mosher and already a successful pieceworker on skirts in Brooklyn. The picture postcards from him of the Statue of Liberty! Of the three of them, Aaron, Gussie, his wife, and little Leo, with donkey bodies sporting down a beach labeled "Coney." A horrific tintype of little Leo in tiny velveteen knickerbockers that fastened with large, ruble-sized, mother-of-pearl buttons up to an embroidered sailor blouse.

It was those mother-of-pearl buttons that captured Sara's imagination so that she loved and wept over the tintype until little Leo quite disappeared under the rust of her tears. Long after young Mosher, who loved his Talmud, had retired to sway over it, Sara could yearn at this tintype.

Her sons in little knickerbockers that fastened to the waistband with large pearl buttons!

Her black-eyed Nikolai with the strong black hair and the virile little profile that hooked against the pillow as he slept.

Her red-headed Schmulka with the tight curls, golden eyes, and even more thrusting profile. So different of feature her twins and yet so temperamentally of a key. Flaming to the same childish passions, often too bitter, she thought, and, trembling with an unnamed fear, would tear them apart.

Pull of the cruelties and the horrible torture complex of the young male, they had once burned a cat alive, and the passion of their father and their cries under flaying had beat about in her brain for weeks after. Jealousies, each of the other, burned fiercely, and, aged three, they scratched blood from one another over the favor of the shoemaker's tot of a girl. And once, to her soul-sickness, Nikolai, the black one, had found out the vodka and drunk of it until she discovered him in a little stupor beside the cupboard.

Yet—and Sara would recount with her eyes full of more tears than they could hold the often-told tale of how Schmulka, who could bear no injustice, championed the cause of little Mottke, the butcher's son, against the onslaught of his drunken father, beating back the lumbering attack with small fists tight with rage; of little Nikolai, who fell down the jagged wall of a quarry and endured a broken arm for the six hours until his father came home rather than burden his mother with what he knew would be the agony of his pain.

Red and black were Sara's sons in pigment. But by the time they were four, almost identical in passion, inflammable both to the same angers, the impulsive and the judiciary cunningly distributed in them.

And so, to the solemn and Talmud teachings of Mosher and the wide-bosomed love of this mother who lavishly nurtured them, these sons, so identically pitched, grew steady of limb, with all the thigh-pulling power of their parents, the calves of their little legs already tight as fists. And from the bookkeeping one snow-smelling night, to the drip-drip of tallow, there came the decisive moment when America looked exactly four months off!

Then one starlit hour before dawn the pogrom broke. Redly, from the very start, because from the first bang of a bayonet upon a door blood began to flow and smell.

There had been rumors. For days old Genendel, the ragpicker, had prophetically been showing about the village the rising knobs of his knotting rheumatic knuckles, ill omen of storm or havoc. A star had shot down one night, as white and sardonic as a Cossack's grin and almost with a hiss behind it. Mosher, returning from a peddling tour to a neighboring village, had worn a furrow between his eyes. Headache, he called it. Somehow Sara vaguely sensed it to be the ache of a fear.

One night there was a furious pink tint on the distant horizon, and borne on miles of the stiffly thin air came the pungency of burning wood and flesh across the snowlight. Flesh! The red sky lay off in the direction of Kishinef. What was it? The straw roof of a burning barn? The precious flesh of an ox? What? Reb Baruch, with a married daughter and eleven children in Kishinef, sat up all night and prayed and swayed and trembled.

Packed in airtight against the bite of the steely out-of-doors, most of the village of Vodna—except the children and the half-witted Shimsha, the *ganef*—huddled under its none-too-plentiful coverings that night and prayed and trembled.

At five o'clock that red dawn, almost as if a bayonet had crashed into her dream, Sara, her face smeared with pallor, awoke to the smell of her own hair singeing. A bayonet *had* crashed, but through the door, terribly!

The rest is an anguished war frieze of fleeing figures; of running hither and thither in the wildness of fear; of mothers running with babes at breasts; of men, their twisted faces steaming sweat, locked in the Laocoön embrace of death. Banners of flame. The exultant belch of iridescent smoke. Cries the shape of steel rapiers. A mouth torn back to an ear. Prayers being moaned. The sticky stench of coagulating blood. Pillage. Outrage. Old men dragging household chattels. Figures crumpling up in the outlandish attitudes of death. The enormous braying of frightened cattle. A spurred heel over a face in that horrible moment when nothing can stay its descent. The shriek of a round-bosomed girl to the smear of wet lips across hers. The superb daring of her lover to kill her. A babe in arms. Two. The black billowing of fireless smoke.

A child in the horse trough, knocked there from its mother's arms by the butt end of a bayonet, its red curls quite sticky in a circle of its little blood. A half-crazed mother with a singed eyebrow, blatting over it and groveling on her breasts toward the stiffening figure for the warmth they could not give; the father, a black-haired child in his arms, tearing her by force out of the zone of buckshot, plunging back into it himself to cover up decently, with his coat, what the horse trough held.

Dawn. A huddle of fugitives. Footsteps of blood across the wide open places of snow. A mother, whose eyes are terrible with what she has left in the horse trough, fighting to turn back. A husband who literally carries her, screaming, farther and farther across the cruel open places. A town. A ship. The crucified eyes of the mother always looking back. Back.

And so it was that Sara and Mosher Turkletaub sailed for America with only one twin—Nikolai, the black.

* * * * *

The Turkletaubs prospered. Turkletaub Brothers, Skirts, the year after the war, paying a six-figure excess-profit tax.

Aaron dwelt in a three-story, American-basement house in West 120th Street, near Lenox Avenue, with his son Leo, office manager of the Turkletaub Skirt Company, and who had recently married the eldest daughter of an exceedingly well-to-do Maiden Lane jewelry merchant.

The Mosher Turkletaubs occupied an eight-room-and-two-baths apartment near by. Sara, with much of the fleetness gone from her face and a smile tempered by a look of unshed tears, marketing now by white-enameled desk telephone or, on days when the limp from an old burn down her thigh was not too troublesome, walked up to a plate-glass butcher shop on 125th Street, where there was not so much as a drop of blood on the marble counter and the fowl hung in white, plucked window display with garnitures of pink tissue paper about the ankles and even the dangling heads wrapped so that the dead eyes might not give offense.

It was a widely different Sara from the water lugger of those sweaty Russian days. Such commonplaces of environment as elevator service, water at the turning of a tap, potatoes dug and delivered to her dumbwaiter, had softened Sara and, it is true, vanquished, along with the years, some of the wing flash of vitality from across her face. So was the tough fiber of her skin vanquished to almost a creaminess, and her hair, due perhaps to the warm water always on tap, had taken on a sheen, and even through its grayness grew out hardily and was well trained to fall in soft scallops over the singed place.

Yes, all in all, life had sweetened Sara, and, except for the occasional look of crucifixion somewhere back in her eyes, had roly-polied her into new rotundities of hip and shelf of bosom, and even to what mischievously promised to be a scallop of second chin.

Sara Turkletaub, daughter of a ne'er-do-well who had died before her birth with the shadow of an unproved murder on him; Sara, who had run swiftly barefoot for the first dozen summers of her life, and married, without dower or approval, the reckless son of old Turkletaub, the peddler; Sara, who once back in the dim years, when a bull had got loose in the public square, had jerked him to a halt by swinging herself from his horns, and later, standing by, had helped hold him for the emergency of an un-kosher slaughter, not even paling at the slitting noises of the knife.

Mosher Turkletaub, who had peddled new feet for stockings and calico for the sacques the peasant women wore in the fields, reckoning no longer in dozens of rubles but in dozens of thousands! Indeed, Turkletaub Brothers could now afford to owe the bank one hundred thousand dollars! Mosher dwelling thus, thighs gone flabby, in a seven-story apartment house with a liveried lackey to swing open the front door and another to shoot him upward in a gilded elevator.

It was to laugh!

And Sara and Mosher with their son, their turbulent Nikolai, now an accredited Doctor of Law and practicing before the bar of the city of New York!

It was upon that realization, most of all, that Sara could surge tears, quickly and hotly, and her heart seem to hurt of fullness.

Of Nikolai, the black. Nicholas, now:

It was not without reason that Sara had cried terrible tears over him, and that much, but not all, of the struggle was gone from her face. Her boy could be as wayward as the fling to his fierce black head, and sickeningly often Mosher, with a nausea at the very pit of him, had wielded the lash.

Once even Nicholas in his adolescent youth, handsomely dark, had stood in Juvenile Court, ringleader of a neighborhood gang of children on a foray into the strange world of some packets of cocaine purloined from the rear of a vacated Chinese laundry.

Bitterly had Mosher stood in the fore of that court room, thumbing his hat, his heart gangrening, and trying in a dumbly miserable sort of way to press down, with his hand on her shoulder, some of the heaving of Sara's enormous tears.

There had followed a long, bitter evening of staying the father's lash from descending, and finally, after five hours with his mother in his little room, her wide bosom the sea wall against which the boiling waywardness of him surged, his high head came down like a black swan's and apparently, at least so far as Mosher knew, Sara had won again.

And so it was that with the bulwark of this mother and a father who spared not the wise rod even at the price of the sickness it cost him, Nicholas came cleanly through these difficult years of the long midchannel of his waywardness.

At twenty-one he was admitted to the bar of the city of New York, although an event so perilous followed it by a year or two that the scallops of strong hair that came down over the singed place of Sara's brow whitened that year; although Mosher, who was beginning to curve slightly of the years as he walked, as if a blow had been struck him from behind, never more than heard the wind before the storm.

Listen in on the following:

The third year that Nicholas practiced law, junior member in the Broad Street firm of Leavitt & Dilsheimer, he took to absenting himself from dinner so frequently, that across the sturdy oak dining table, laid out in a red-and-white cloth, gold-band china not too thick of lip, and a cut-glass fern dish with cunningly contrived cotton carnations stuck in among the growing green, Sara, over rich and native foods, came more and more to regard her husband through a clutch of fear.

"I tell you, Mosher, something has come over the boy. It ain't like him to miss *gefülte*-fish supper three Fridays in succession."

"All right, then, because he has a few more or less *gefülte*-fish suppers in his life, let it worry you! If that ain't a woman every time."

"*Gefülte* fish! If that was my greatest worry. But it's not so easy to prepare, that you should take it so much for granted. *Gefülte* fish, he says, just like it grew on trees and didn't mean two hours' chopping on my feet."

"Now, Sara, was that anything to fly off at? Do I ever so much as eat two helpings of it in Gussie's house? That's how I like yours better!"

"Gussie don't chop up her onions fine enough. A hundred times I tell her and a hundred times she does them coarse. Her own daughter-in-law, a girl that was raised in luxury, can cook better as Gussie. I tell you, Mosher, I take off my hat to those Berkowitz girls. And if you should ask me, Ada is a finer one even than Leo's Irma."

The sly look of wiseacre wizened up Mosher's face.

"Ada!" she says. "The way you pronounce that girl's name, Sara, it's like every tooth in your mouth was diamond filled out of Berkowitz's jewelry firm."

Quite without precedent Sara's lips began to quiver at this pleasantry.

"I'm worried, Mosher," she said, putting down a forkful of untasted food that had journeyed twice toward her lips. "I don't say he—Nicky—I don't say he should always stay home evenings when Ada comes over sometimes with Leo and Irma, but night after night—three times whole nights—I—Mosher, I'm afraid."

In his utter well-being from her warming food, Mosher drank deeply and, if it must be admitted, swishingly, through his mustache, inhaling copiously the draughts of Sara's coffee.

Do not judge from the mustache cup with the gilt "Papa" inscribed, that Sara's home did not meticulously reflect the newer McKinley period, so to speak, of the cut-glass-china closet, curio cabinet, brass bedstead, velour upholstery, and the marbelette Psyche.

They had furnished newly three years before, the year the business almost doubled, Sara and Gussie simultaneously, the two of them poring with bibliophiles' fervor over Grand Rapids catalogic literature.

Bravely had Sara, even more so than Gussie, sacrificed her old regime to the dealer. Only a samovar remained. A red-and-white pressed-glass punch bowl, purchased out of Nicholas's—aged fourteen—pig-bank savings. An enlarged crayon of her twins from a baby picture. A patent rocker which she kept in the kitchen. (It fitted her so for the attitude of peeling.) Two bisque plaques, with embossed angels. Another chair capable of metamorphosis into a ladder. And Mosher's cup.

From this Mosher drank with gusto. His mustache, to Sara so thrillingly American, without its complement of beard, could flare so above the relishing sounds of drinking. It flared now and Mosher would share none of her concern.

"You got two talents, Sara. First, for being my wife; and second, for wasting worry like it don't cost you nothing in health or trips to Cold Springs in the Catskills for the baths. Like it says in Nicky's Shakespeare, a boy who don't sow his wild oats when he's young will some day do 'em under another name that don't smell so sweet."

"I—It ain't like I can talk over Nicky with you, Mosher, like another woman could with her husband. Either you give him right or right away you get so mad you make it worse with him than better."

"Now, Sara—"

"But only this morning that Mrs. Lessauer I meet sometimes at Epstein's fish store—you know the rich sausage-casings Lessauers—she says to me this morning, she says with her sweetness full of such a meanness, like it was knives in me—'Me and my son and daughter-in-law was coming out of a movie last night and we saw your son getting into a taxicab with such a blonde in a red hat!' The way she said it, Mosher, like a cat licking its whiskers—'such a blonde in a red hat'!"

"I wish I had one dollar in my pocket for every blond hat with red hair her Felix had before he married."

"But it's the second time this week I hear it, Mosher. The same description of such a—a nix in a red hat. Once in a cabaret show Gussie says she heard it from a neighbor, and now in and out from taxicabs with her. Four times this week he's not been home, Mosher. I can't help it, I—I get crazy with worry."

A sudden, almost a simian old-age seemed to roll, like a cloud that can thunder, across Sara's face. She was suddenly very small and no little old. Veins came out on her brow and upon the backs of her hands, and Mosher, depressed with an unconscious awareness, was looking into the tired, cold, watery eyes of the fleet woman who had been his.

"Why, Sara!" he said, and came around the table to let her head wilt in unwonted fashion against his coat. "Mamma!"

"I'm tired, Mosher." She said her words almost like a gush of warm blood from the wound of her mouth. "I'm tired from keeping up and holding in. I have felt so sure for these last four years that we have saved him from his—his wildness—and now, to begin all over again, I—I 'ain't got the fight left in me, Mosher."

"You don't have to have any fight in you, Mamma. 'Ain't you got a husband and a son to fight for you?"

"Sometimes I think, except for the piece of my heart I left lying back there, that there are worse agonies than even massacres. I've struggled so that he should be good and great, Mosher, and now, after four years already thinking I've won—maybe, after all, I haven't."

"Why, Sara! Why, Mamma! Shame! I never saw you like this before. You ain't getting sick for another trip to the Catskills, are you? Maybe you need some baths—"

"Sulphur water don't cure heart sickness."

"Heart sickness, nonsense! You know I don't always take sides with Nicky, Mamma. I don't say he hasn't been a hard boy to raise. But a man, Mamma, is a man! I wouldn't think much of him if he wasn't. You 'ain't got him to your apron string in short pants any more. Whatever troubles we've had with him, women haven't been one of them. Shame, Mamma, the first time your grown-up son of a man cuts up maybe a little nonsense with the girls! Shame!"

"Girls! No one would want more than me he should settle himself down to a fine, self-respecting citizen with a fine, sweet girl like Ad—"

"Believe me, and I ain't ashamed to say it, I wasn't an angel, neither, every minute before I was married."

"My husband brags to me about his indiscretioncies."

"*Na, na*, Mamma, right away when I open my mouth you make out a case against me. I only say it to show you how a mother maybe don't understand as well as a father how natural a few wild oats can be."

"L-Leo didn't have 'em."

"Leo ain't a genius. He's just a good boy."

"I—I worry so!"

"Sara, I ask you, wouldn't I worry, too, if there was a reason? God forbid if his nonsense should lead to really something serious, then it's time to worry."

Sara Turkletaub dried her eyes, but it was as if the shadow of crucifixion had moved forward in them.

"If just once, Mosher, Nicky would make it easy for me, like Leo did for Gussie. When Leo's time comes he marries a fine girl like Irma Berkowitz from a fine family, and has fine children, without Gussie has to cry her eyes out first maybe he's in company that—that—"

"I don't say, Sara, we didn't have our hard times with your boy. But we got results enough that we shouldn't complain. Maybe you're right. With a boy like Leo, a regular good business head who comes into the firm with us, it ain't been such a strain for Gussie and Aaron as for us with a genius. But neither have they got the smart son, the lawyer of the family, for theirs. *We* got a temperament in ours, Sara. Ain't that something to be proud of?"

She laid her cheek to his lapel, the freshet of her tears past staying.

"I—I know it, Mosher. It ain't—often I give way like this."

"We got such results as we can be proud of, Sara. A genius of a lawyer son on his way to the bench. Mark my word if I ain't right, on his way to the bench!"

"Yes, yes, Mosher."

"Well then, Sara, I ask you, is it nice to—"

"I know it, Papa. I ought to be ashamed. Instead of me fighting you to go easy with the boy, this time it's you fighting me. If only he—he was the kind of boy I could talk this out with, it wouldn't worry me so. When it comes to—to a girl—it's so different. It's just that I'm tired, Mosher. If anything was to go wrong after all these years of struggling for him—alone—"

"Alone! Alone! Why, Sara! Shame! Time after time for punishing him I was a sick man!"

"That's it! That's why so much of it was alone. I don't know why I should say it all to-night after—after so many years of holding in."

"Say what?"

"You meant well, God knows a father never meant better, but it wasn't the way to handle our boy's nature with punishments, and a quick temper like yours. Your way was wrong, Mosher, and I knew it. That's why so much of it was—alone—so much that I had to contend with I was afraid to tell you, for fear—for fear—"

"Now, now, Mamma, is that the way to cry your eyes out about nothing? I don't say I'm not sometimes hasty—"

"Time and time again—keeping it in from you—after the Chinese laundry that night after you—you whipped him so—you never knew the months of nights with him afterward—when I found out he liked that—stuff! Me alone with him—"

"Sara, is now time to rake up such ten-year-old nonsense!"

"It's all coming out in me now, Mosher. The strain. You never knew. That time you had to send me to the Catskills for the baths. You thought it was rheumatism. I knew what was the matter with me. Worry. The nights—Mosher. He liked it. I found it hid away in the toes of his gymnasium shoes and in the mouth to his bugle. He—liked that stuff, Mosher. You didn't know that, did you?"

"Liked what?"

"It. The—the stuff from the Chinese laundry. Even after the Juvenile Court, when you thought it was all over after the whipping that night. He'd snuff it up. I found him twice on his bed after school. All druggy-like—half sleeping and half laughing. The gang at school he was in with—learned him—"

"You mean—?"

"It ain't so easy to undo with a day in Juvenile Court such a habit like that. You thought the court was the finish. My fight just began then!"

"Why, Sara!"

"You remember the time he broke his kneecap and how I fighted the doctors against the hypodermic and you got so mad because I wouldn't let him have it to ease the pain. I knew why it was better he should suffer than have it. *I knew!* It was a long fight I had with him alone, Mosher. He liked that—stuff."

"That—don't—seem possible."

"And that wasn't the only lead-pipe case that time, neither, Mosher. Twice I had to lay out of my own pocket so you wouldn't know, and talk to him 'til sometimes I thought I didn't have any more tears left inside of me. Between you and your business worries that year of the garment-workers' strike—and our boy—I—after all that I haven't got the strength left. Now that he's come out of it big, I can't begin over again. I haven't got what he would call the second wind for it. If anything should keep him now from going straight ahead to make him count as a citizen, I wouldn't have the strength left to fight it, Mosher. Wouldn't!"

And so Sara Turkletaub lay back with the ripple writing of stormy high tides crawling out in wrinkles all over her face and her head, that he had never seen low, wilting there against his breast.

He could not be done with soothing her, his own face suddenly as puckered as an old shoe, his chin like the toe curling up.

"Mamma, Mamma, I didn't know! God knows I never dreamt—"

"I know you didn't, Mosher. I ain't mad. I'm only tired. I 'ain't got the struggle left in me. This feeling won't last in me, I'll be all right, but I'm tired, Mosher—so tired."

"My poor Sara!"

"And frightened. Such a blonde in a red hat. Cabarets. Taxicabs. Night after night. Mosher, hold me. I'm frightened."

Cheek to cheek in their dining room of too-carved oak, twin shadow-boxed paintings of Fruit and Fish, the cut-glass punch bowl with the hooked-on cups, the cotton palm, casually rigid velour drapes, the elusive floor bell, they huddled, these two, whose eyes were branded with the scars of what they had looked upon, and a slow, a vast anger began to rise in Mosher, as if the blood in his throat were choking him, and a surge of it, almost purple, rose out of his collar and stained his face.

"Loafer! Low-life! No-'count! His whole body ain't worth so much as your little finger. I'll learn him to be a worry to you with this all-night business. By God! I'll learn my loafer of a son to—"

On the pistol shot of that, Sara's body jumped out of its rigidity, all her faculties coiled to spring.

"He isn't! You know he isn't! 'Loafer'! Shame on you! Whatever else he is, he's not a loafer. Boys will be boys—you say so yourself. 'Loafer'! You should know once what some parents go through with real *loafers* for sons—"

"No child what brings you such worry is anything else than a loafer!"

"And I say 'no'! The minute I so much as give you a finger in finding fault with that boy, right away you take a hand!"

"I'll break his—"

"You don't know yet a joke when you hear one. I wanted to get you mad! I get a little tired and I try to make myself funny."

"There wasn't no funniness in the way your eyes looked when you—"

"I tell you I didn't mean one word. No matter what uneasiness that child has brought me, always he has given me more in happiness. Twice more. That's what he's been. Twice of everything to make up for—for only being half of my twins."

"Then what the devil is—"

"I don't envy Gussie her Leo and his steady ways. Didn't you say yourself for a boy like ours you got to pay with a little uneasiness?"

"Not when that little uneasiness is enough to make his mother sick."

"Sick! If I felt any better I'd be ashamed of having so much health! If you get mad with him and try to ask him where he stays every night is all that can cause me worry. It's natural a handsome boy like ours should sow what they call his wild oat. With such a matzos face like poor Leo, from where he broke his nose, I guess it ain't so easy for him to have his wild oat. Promise me, Mosher, you won't ask one question or get mad at him. His mother knows how to handle her boy so he don't even know he's handled."

"I'll handle him—"

"See now, just look at yourself once in the glass with your eyes full of red. That's why I can't tell you nothing. Right away you fly to pieces. I say again, you don't know how to handle your son. Promise me you won't say nothing to him or let on, Mosher. Promise me."

"That's the way with you women. You get a man crazy and then—"

"I tell you it's just my nonsense."

"If I get mad you're mad, and if I don't get mad you're mad! Go do me something to help me solve such a riddle like you."

"It's because me and his aunt Gussie are a pair of matchmaking old women. That the two cousins should marry the two sisters, Irma and Ada, we got it fixed between us! Just as if because we want it that way it's got to happen that way!"

"A pair of geeses, the two of you!"

"I wouldn't let on to Gussie, but Ada, the single one, has got Leo's Irma beat for looks. Such a complexion! And the way she comes over to sew with me afternoons! A young girl like that! An old woman like me! You see, Mosher? See?"

"See, she asks me. What good does it do me if I see or I don't see when his mother gets her mind made up?"

"But does Nicky so much as look at her? That night at Leo's birthday I was ashamed the way he right away had an engagement after supper, when she sat next to him and all through the meal gave him the white meat off her own plate. Why, the flowered chiffon dress that girl had on cost ten dollars a yard if it cost a cent. Did Nicky so much as look at her? No."

"Too many birthdays in this family."

"I notice you eat them when they are set down in front of you!"

"Eat what?"

"The birthdays."

"Ha! That's fine! A new dish. Boiled birthdays with horseradish sauce."

"All right, then, the birthday *parties*. Don't be so exactly with me. Many a turn in his grave you yourself have given the man who made the dictionary. I got other worries than language. If I knew where he is—to-night—"

Rather contentedly, while Sara cleared and tidied, Mosher snapped open his evening paper, drawing his spectacles down from the perch of his forehead.

"You women," he said, breathing out with the male's easy surcease from responsibility—"you women and your worries. If you 'ain't got 'em, you make 'em."

"Heigh-ho!" sighed out Sara, presently, having finished, and diving into her open workbasket for the placidity her flying needle could so cunningly simulate. "Heigh-ho!"

But inside her heart was beating over and over again to itself, rapidly:

"If—only-I—knew—where—he—is—to—night—if—only—I—knew—where —he—is—to—night."

II

This is where he was:

In the Forty-fifth-Street flat of Miss Josie Drew, known at various times and places as Hattie Moore, Hazel Derland, Mrs. Hazel, and—But what does it matter.

At this writing it was Josie Drew of whom more is to be said of than for.

Yet pause to consider the curve of her clay. Josie had not molded her nose. Its upward fling was like the brush of a perfumed feather duster to the senses. Nor her mouth. It had bloomed seductively, long before her lip stick rushed to its aid and abetment, into a cherry at the bottom of a glass for which men quaffed deeply. There was something rather terrifyingly inevitable about her. Just as the tide is plaything of the stars, so must the naughty turn to Josie's ankle have been complement to the naughty turn of her mind.

It is not easy for the woman with a snub nose and lips molded with a hard pencil to bleed the milk of human kindness over the frailties of the fruity chalice that contained Miss Drew. She could not know, for instance, if her own gaze was merely owlish and thin-lashed, the challenge of eyes that are slightly too long. Miss Drew did. Simply drooping hers must have stirred her with a none-too-nice sense of herself, like the swell of his biceps can bare the teeth of a gladiator.

That had been the Josie Drew of eighteen.

At thirty she penciled the droop to her eyebrows a bit and had a not always successful trick of powdering out the lurking caves under her eyes. There was even a scar, a peculiar pocking of little shotted spots as if glass had ground in, souvenir of one out of dozens of such nights of orgies, this particular one the result of some unmentionable jealousy she must have coaxed to the surface.

She wore it plastered over with curls. It was said that in rage it turned green. But who knows? It was also said that Josie Drew's correct name was Josie Rosalsky. But again who knows? Her past was vivid with the heat lightning of the sharp storms of men's lives. At nineteen she had worn in public restaurants a star-sapphire necklace, originally designed by a soap magnate for his wife, of these her birthstones.

At twenty her fourteen-room apartment faced the Park, but was on the ground floor because a vice-president of a bank, a black-broadcloth little pelican of a man, who stumped on a cane and had a pink tin roof to his mouth, disliked elevators.

At twenty-three and unmentionably enough, a son of a Brazilian coffee king, inflamed with the deviltry of debauch, had ground a wine tumbler against her forehead, inducing the pock marks. At twenty-seven it was the fourth vice-president of a Harlem bank. At twenty-nine an interim. Startling to Josie Drew. Terrifying. Lean. For the first time in eight years her gasoline expenditures amounted to ninety cents a month instead of from forty to ninety dollars. And then not at the garage, but at the corner drug store. Cleaning fluid for kicked-out glove and slipper tips.

The little jangle of chatelaine absurdities which she invariably affected— mesh bag, lip stick, memorandum (for the traffic in telephone numbers), vanity, and cigarette case were gold—filled. There remained a sapphire necklace, but this one faithfully copied to the wink of the stars and the pearl clasp by the Chemic Jewel Company. Much of the indoor appeal of Miss Drew was still the pink silkiness of her, a little stiffened from washing and ironing, it is true, but there was a flesh-colored arrangement of intricate drape that was rosily kind to her. Also a vivid yellow one of a later and less expensive period, all heavily slashed in Valenciennes lace. This brought out a bit of virago through her induced blondness, but all the same it italicized her, just as the crescent of black court plaster exclaimed at the whiteness of her back.

She could spend an entire morning fluffing at these things, pressing out, with a baby electric iron and a sleeve board, a crumple of chiffon to new sheerness, getting at spots with cleaning fluid. Under alcoholic duress Josie dropped things. There was a furious stain down the yellow, from a home brew of canned lobster á la Newburg. The stain she eliminated entirely by cutting out the front panel and wearing it skimpier.

In these first slanting years, in her furnished flat of upright, mandolin-attachment piano, nude plaster-of-Paris Bacchante holding a cluster of pink-glass incandescent grapes, divan mountainous with scented pillows, she was about as obvious as a gilt slipper that has started to rub, or a woman's kiss that is beery and leaves a red imprint.

To Nicholas Turkletaub, whose adolescence had been languid and who had never known a woman with a fling, a perfume, or a moue (there had been only a common-sense-heeled co-ed of his law-school days and the rather plump little sister-in-law of Leo's), the dawn of Josie cleft open something in his consciousness, releasing maddened perceptions that stung his eyeballs. He sat in the imitation cheap frailty of her apartment like a young bull with threads of red in his eyeballs, his head, not unpoetic with its shag of black hair, lowered as if to bash at the impotence of the thing she aroused in him.

Also, a curious thing had happened to Josie. Something so jaded in her that she thought it long dead, was stirring sappily, as if with springtime.

Maybe it was a resurgence of sense of power after months of terror that the years had done for her.

At any rate, it was something strangely and deeply sweet.

"Nicky-boy," she said, sitting on the couch with her back against the wall, her legs out horizontally and clapping her rubbed gilt slippers together—"Nicky-boy must go home ten o'clock to-night. Josie-girl tired."

Her mouth, like a red paper rose that had been crushed there, was always bunched to baby talk.

"Come here," he said, and jerked her so that the breath jumped.

"Won't," she said, and came.

His male prowess was enormous to him. He could bend her back almost double with a kiss, and did. His first kisses that he spent wildly. He could have carried her off like Persephone's bull, and wanted to, so swift his mood. His flare for life and for her leaped out like a flame, and something precious that had hardly survived sixteen seemed to stir in the early grave of her heart.

"Oh, Nicky-boy! Nicky-boy!" she said, and he caught that she was yearning over him.

"Don't say it in down curves like that. Say it up. Up."

She didn't get this, but, with the half-fearful tail of her eye for the clock, let him hold her quiescent, while the relentlessly sliding moments ticked against her unease.

"I'm jealous of every hour you lived before I met you."

"Big-bad-eat-Josie-up-boy!"

"I want to kiss your eyes until they go in deep—through you—I don't know—until they hurt—deep—I—want—to hurt you—"

"Oh! Oh! Josie scared!"

"You're like one of those orange Angora kittens. Yellow. Soft. Deep."

"I Nicky's pussy."

"I can see myself in your eyes. Shut me up in them."

"Josie so tired."

"Of me?"

"Nicky so—so strong."

"My poor pussy! I didn't mean—"

"Nicky-boy, go home like good Nicky."

"I don't want ever to go home."

"Go now, Josie says."

"You mean never."

"Now!"

He kissed his "No, No," down against each of her eyelids.

"You must," she said this time, and pushed him off.

For a second he sat quite still, the black shine in his eyes seeming to give off diamond points.

"You're nervous," he said, and jerked her back so that the breath jumped again.

The tail of her glance curved to the gilt clock half hidden behind a litter of used highball glasses, and then, seeing that his quickly suspicious eye followed hers:

"No," she said, "not nervous. Just tired—and thirsty."

He poured her a high drink from a decanter, and held it so that, while she sipped, her teeth were magnified through the tumbler, and he thought that adorable and tilted the glass higher against her lips, and when she choked soothed her with a crush of kisses.

"You devil," he said, "everything you do maddens me."

There was a step outside and a scraping noise at the lock. It was only a vaudeville youth, slender as a girl, who lived on the floor above, feeling unsteadily, and a bit the worse for wear, for the lock that must eventually fit his key.

But on that scratch into the keyhole, Josie leaped up in terror, so that Nicholas went staggering back against the Bacchante, shattering to a fine ring of crystal some of the pink grapes, and on that instant she clicked out the remaining lights, shoving him, with an unsuspected and catamount strength, into an adjoining box of a kitchenette.

There an uncovered bulb burned greasily over a small refrigerator, that stood on a table and left only the merest slit of walking space. It was the none too fastidious kitchen of a none too fastidious woman. A pair of dress shields hung on the improvised clothesline of a bit of twine. A clump of sardines, one end still shaped to the tin, cloyed in its own oil, crumbily, as if bread had been sopped in, the emptied tin itself, with the top rolled back with a patent key, filled now with old beer. Obviously the remaining contents of a tumbler had been flung in. Cigarette stubs floated. A pasteboard cylindrical box, labeled "Sodium Bi-carbonate," had a spoon stuck in it. A rubber glove drooped deadly over the sink edge.

On the second that he stood in that smelling fog, probably for no longer than it took the swinging door to settle, something of sickness rushed over Nicholas. The unaired odors of old foods. Those horrific things on the line. The oil that had so obviously been sopped up with bread. The old beer, edged in grease. Something of sickness and a panoramic flash of things absurdly, almost unreasonably irrelevant.

Snow, somewhere back in his memory. A frozen silence of it that was clean and thin to the smell. The ridges in the rattan with which his father had whipped him the night after the Chinese laundry. The fine white head of the dean of the law school. His mother baking for Friday night in a blue-and-white gingham apron that enveloped her. Red curls—some one's—somewhere. The string of tiny Oriental pearls that rose and fell with the little pouter-pigeon swell of a bosom. Pretty perturbation. His cousin's sister-in-law, Ada. A small hole in a pink-silk stocking, peeping like a little rising sun above the heel of a rubbed gilt slipper. Josie's slipper.

Something seemed suddenly to rise in Nicholas, with the quick capillarity of water boiling over.

The old familiar star-spangled red over which Sara had time after time laid sedative hand against his seeing, sprang out. The pit of his passion was bottomless, into which he was tumbling with the icy laughter of breaking glass.

Then he struck out against the swinging door so that it ripped outward with a sough of stale air, striking Josie Drew, as she approached it from the room side, so violently that her teeth bit down into her lips and the tattling blood began to flow.

"Nicky! It's a mistake. I thought—my sister—It got so late—you wouldn't go. Go now! The key—turning—Nervous—silly—mistake. Go—"

He laughed, something exhilarant in his boiling over, and even in her sudden terror of him she looked at his bare teeth and felt the unnice beauty of the storm.

"Nicky," she half cried, "don't be—foolish! I—"

And then he struck her across the lip so that her teeth cut in again.

"There is some one coming here to-night," he said, with his smile still very white.

She sat on the couch, trying to bravado down her trembling.

"And what if there is? He'll beat you up for this! You fool! I've tried to explain a dozen times. You know, or if you don't you ought to, that there's a—friend. A traveling salesman. Automobile accessories. Long trips, but good money. Good money. And here you walk in a few weeks ago and expect to find the way clear! Good boy, you like some one to go ahead of you with a snow cleaner, don't you? Yes, there's some one due in here off his trip to-night. What's the use trying to tell Nicky-boy with his hot head. He's got a hot head, too. Go, and let me clear the way for you, Nicky. For good if you say the word. But I have to know where I'm at. Every girl does if she wants to keep her body and soul together. You don't let me know where I stand. You know you've got me around your little finger for the saying, but you don't say. Only go now, Nicky-boy. For God's sake, it's five minutes to eleven and he's due in on that ten-forty-five. Nicky-boy, go, and come back to me at six to-morrow night. I'll have the way clear then, for good. Quit blinking at me like that, Nicky. You scare me! Quit! When you come back to-morrow evening there won't be any more going home for Josie's Nicky-boy. Nicky, go now. He's hotheaded, too. Quit blinking, Nicky—for God's sake—Nicky—"

It was then Nicholas bent back her head as he did when he kissed her there on the swan's arch to her neck, only this time his palm was against her forehead and his other between her shoulder blades.

"I could kill you," he said, and laughed with his teeth. "I could bend back your neck until it breaks."

"Ni—i—Nic—ky—"

"And I want to," he said through the star-spangled red. "I want you to crack when I twist. I'm going to twist—twist—"

And he did, shoving back her hair with his palm, and suddenly bared, almost like a grimace, up at him, was the glass-shotted spot where the wine tumbler had ground in, greenish now, like the flanges of her nostrils.

Somewhere—down a dear brow was a singed spot like that—singed with the flame of pain—

"Nicky, for God's sake—you're—you're spraining my neck! Let go! Nicky. God! if you hadn't let go just when you did. You had me croaking. Nicky-boy—kiss me now and go! Go! To-morrow at six—clear for you—always—only go—please, boy—my terrible—my wonderful. To-morrow at six."

Somehow he was walking home, the burn of her lips still against his, loathsome and gorgeous to his desires. He wanted to tear her out by the roots from his consciousness. To be rollickingly, cleanly free of her. His teeth shone against the darkness as he walked, drenched to the skin of his perspiration and one side of his collar loose, the buttonhole slit.

Rollickingly free of her and yet how devilishly his shoes could clat on the sidewalk.

To-morrow at six. To-morrow at six. To-morrow at six.

* * * * *

It was some time after midnight when he let himself into the uptown apartment. He thought he heard his mother, trying to be swift, padding down the hallway as if she had been waiting near the door. That would have angered him.

The first of these nights, only four weeks before (it seemed years), he had come in hotly about four o'clock and gone to bed. About five he thought he heard sounds, almost like the scratch of a little dog at his door. He sprang up and flung it open. The flash of his mother's gray-flannelette wrapper turned a corner of the hall. She must have been crying out there and wanting him to need her. None the less it had angered him. These were men's affairs.

But in his room to-night the light burned placidly on the little table next to the bed, a glass of milk on a plate beside it. The bed was turned back, snowy sheets forming a cool envelope for him to slip in between. The room lay sedatively in shadow. A man's room. Books, uncurving furniture, photographs of his parents taken on their twenty-fifth anniversary standing on the chiffonier in a double leather frame that opened like a book. Face down on the reading table beside the glass of milk, quite as he must have left it the night before, except where Sara had lifted it to dust under, a copy of Bishop's *New Criminal Law*, already a prognosis, as it were, of that branch of the law he was ultimately and brilliantly to bend to fuller justice.

Finally, toward morning Nicholas slept, and at ten o'clock of a rain-swept Sunday forenoon awoke, as he knew he must, to the grip of a blinding headache, so called for want of a better noun to interpret the kind of agony which, starting somewhere around his eyes, could prick each nerve of his body into a little flame, as if countless matches had been struck.

As a youngster these attacks had not been infrequent, usually after a fit of crying. The first, in fact, had followed the burning of the cat; a duet of twin spasms then, howled into Sara's apron, And once after he had fished an exhausted comrade out of an ice hole in Bronx Park. They had followed the lead-pipe affairs and the Chinese-laundry episode with dreadful inevitability. But it had been five years since the last—the night his mother had fainted with terror at what she had found concealed in the toes of his gymnasium shoes.

Incredible that into his manhood should come the waving specter of those early passions.

At eleven o'clock, after she heard him up and moving about, his mother carried him his kiss and his coffee, steaming black, the way he liked it. She had wanted to bring him an egg—in fact, had prepared one, to just his liking of two minutes and thirty seconds—but had thought better of it, and wisely, because he drank the coffee at a quick gulp and set down the cup with his mouth wry and his eyes squeezed tight. From the taste of it he remembered horridly the litter of tall glasses beside the gilt clock.

With all her senses taut not to fuss around him with little jerks and pullings, Sara jerked and pulled. Too well she knew that furrow between his eyes and wanted unspeakably to tuck him back into bed, lower the shades, and prepare him a vile mixture good for exactly everything that did not ail him. But Sara could be wise even with her son. So instead she flung up the shade, letting him wince at the clatter, dragged off the bedclothes into a tremendous heap on the chair, beat up the pillows, and turned the mattress with a single-handed flop.

"The Sunday-morning papers are in the dining room, son."

"Uhm!"

He was standing in his dressing gown at the rain-lashed window, strumming. Lean, long, and, to Sara, godlike, with the thick shock of his straight hair still wet from the shower.

"Mrs. Berkowitz telephoned already this morning with such a grand compliment for you, son. Her brother-in-law, Judge Rosen, says you're the brains of your firm even if you are only the junior partner yet, and your way looks straight ahead for big things."

"Uhm! Who's talking out there so incessantly, mother?"

"That's your uncle Aaron. He came over for Sunday-morning breakfast with your father. You should see the way he tracked up my hall with his wet shoes. I'm sending him right back home with your father. They should clutter up your aunt Gussie's house with their pinochle and ashes. I had 'em last Sunday.

She don't need to let herself off so easy every week. It's enough if I ask them all over here for supper to-night. Not?"

"Don't count on me, dear. I won't be home for supper."

There was a tom-tom to the silence against her beating ear drums.

"All right, son," she said, pulling her lips until they smiled at him, "with Leo and Irma that'll only make six of us, then."

He kissed her, but so tiredly that again it was almost her irresistible woman's impulse to drag down that fiercely black head to the beating width of her bosom and plead from him drop by drop some of the bitter welling of pain she could see in his eyes.

"Nicky," she started to cry, and then, at his straightening back from her, "come out in the dining room after I pack off the men. I got my work to do. That nix of a house girl left last night. Such sass, too! I'm better off doing my work alone."

Sara, poor dear, could not keep a servant, and, except for the instigation of her husband and son, preferred not to. Cooks rebelled at the exactitude of her household and her disputative reign of the kitchen.

"I'll be out presently, mother," he said, and flung himself down in the leather Morris chair, lighting his pipe and ostensibly settling down to the open-faced volume of *Criminal Law*.

Sara straightened a straight chair. She knew, almost as horridly as if she had looked in on it, the mucky thing that was happening; the intuitive sixth sense of her hovered over him with great wings that wanted to spread. Josie Drew was no surmise with her. The blond head and the red hat were tatooed in pain on her heart and she trembled in a bath of fear, and, trembling, smiled and went out.

Sitting there while the morning ticked on, head thrown back, eyes closed, and all the little darting nerves at him, the dawn of Nicholas Turkletaub's repugnance was all for self. The unfrowsy room, and himself fresh from his own fresh sheets. His mother's eyes with that clean-sky quality in them. The affectionate wrangling of those two decent voices from the dining room. Books! His books, that he loved. His tastiest dream of mother, with immensity and grandeur in her eyes, listening from a privileged first-row bench to the supreme quality of his mercy. *Judge*—Turkletaub!

But tastily, too, and undeniably against his lips, throughout these conjurings, lay the last crushy kiss of Josie Drew. That swany arch to her neck as he bent it back. He had kissed her there. Countlessly.

He tried to dwell on his aversions for her. She had once used an expletive in his presence that had sickened him, and, noting its effect, she had not reiterated. The unfastidious brunette roots to her light hair. That sink with the grease-rimmed old beer! But then: her eyes where the brows slid down to make them heavy-lidded. That bit of blue vein in the crotch of her elbow. That swany arch.

Back somewhere, as the tidy morning wore in, the tranced, the maddening repetition began to tick itself through:

"Six o'clock. Six o'clock."

He rushed out into the hallway and across to the parlor pinkly lit with velours, even through the rainy day, and so inflexibly calm. Sara might have measured the distance between the chairs, so regimental they stood. The pink-velour curlicue divan with the two pink, gold-tasseled cushions, carelessly exact. The onyx-topped table with the pink-velour drape, also gold-tasseled. The pair of equidistant and immaculate china cuspidors, rose-wreathed. The smell of Sunday.

"Nicky, that you?"

It was his mother, from the dining room.

"Yes, mother," and sauntered in.

There were two women sitting at the round table, shelling nuts. One of them his mother, the other Miss Ada Berkowitz, who jumped up, spilling hulls.

Nicholas, in the velveteen dressing gown with the collar turned up, started to back out, Mrs. Turkletaub spoiling that.

"You can come in, Nicky. Ada'll excuse you. I guess she's seen a man in his dressing gown before; the magazine advertisements are full with them in worse and in less. And on Sunday with a headache from all week working so hard, a girl can forgive. He shouldn't think with his head so much, I always tell him, Ada."

"I didn't know he was here," said Miss Berkowitz, already thinking in terms of what she might have worn.

"I telephoned over for Ada, Nicky. They got an automobile and she don't need to get her feet wet to come over to a lonesome old woman on a rainy Sunday, to spend the day and learn me how to make those delicious stuffed dates like she fixed for her mother's card party last week. Draw up a chair, Nicky, and help."

She was casual, she was matter-of-fact, she was bent on the business of nut cracking. They crashed softly, never so much as bruised by her carefully even pressure.

"Thanks," said Nicholas, and sat down, not caring to, but with good enough grace. He wanted his coat, somehow, and fell to strumming the table top.

"Don't, Nicky; you make me nervous."

"Here," said Miss Berkowitz, and gave him a cracker and a handful of nuts. The little crashings resumed.

Ada had very fair skin against dark hair, slightly too inclined to curl. There was quite a creamy depth to her—a wee pinch could raise a bruise. The kind of whiteness hers that challenged the string of tiny Oriental pearls she wore at her throat. Her healthily pink cheeks and her little round bosom were plump, and across the back of each of her hands were four dimples that flashed in and out as she bore down on the cracker. She was as clear as a mountain stream.

"A trifle too plumpy," he thought, but just the same wished he had wet his military brushes.

"Ada has just been telling me, Nicky, about her ambition to be an interior decorator for the insides of houses. I think it is grand the way some girls that are used to the best of everything prepare themselves for, God forbid, they should ever have to make their own livings. I give them credit for it. Tell Nicky, Ada, about the drawing you did last week that your teacher showed to the class."

"Oh," said Ada, blushing softly, "Mr. Turkletaub isn't interested in that."

"Yes, I am," said Nicholas, politely, eating one of the meats.

"You mean the Tudor dining room—"

No, no! You know, the blue-and-white one you said you liked best of all."

"It was a nursery," began Ada, softly. "Just one of those blue-and-white darlingnesses for somebody's little darling."

"For somebody's little darling," repeated Mrs. Turkletaub, silently. She had the habit, when moved, of mouthing people's words after them.

"My idea was—Oh, it's so silly to be telling it again, Mrs. Turkletaub!"

"Silly! I think it's grand that a girl brought up to the best should want to make something of herself. Don't you, Nick?"

"H-m-m!"

"Well, my little idea was white walls with little Delft-blue borders of waddling duckies; white dotted Swiss curtains in the brace of sunny southern-exposure windows, with little Delft-blue borders of more waddling duckies; and dear little nursery rhymes painted in blue on the headboard to keep baby's dreams sweet."

"—baby's dreams sweet! I ask you, is that cute, Nick? Baby's dreams she even interior decorates."

"My—instructor liked that idea, too. He gave me 'A' on the drawing."

"He should have given you the whole alphabet. And tell him about the chairs, Ada. Such originality."

"Oh, Mrs. Turkletaub, that was just a—a little—idea—"

"The modesty of her! Believe me, if it was mine, I'd call it a big one. Tell him."

"Mummie and daddie chairs I call them."

Sara (mouthing): "Mummie and daddie—"

"Two white-enamel chairs to stand on either side of the crib so when mummie and daddie run up in their evening clothes to kiss baby good night—Oh, I just mean two pretty white chairs, one for mummie and one for daddie." Little crash.

"I ask you, Nicky, is that poetical? 'So when mummie and daddie run up to kiss baby good night.' I remember once in Russia, Nicky, all the evening clothes we had was our nightgowns, but when you and your little twin brother were two and a half years old, one night I—"

"Mrs. Turkletaub, did you have twins?"

"Did I have twins, Nicky, she asks me. She didn't know you were twins. A red one I had, as red as my black one is black. You see my Nicky how black and mad-looking he is even when he's glad; well, just so—"

"Now, mother!"

"Just so beautiful and fierce and red was my other beautiful baby. You didn't know, Ada, that a piece of my heart, the red of my blood, I left lying out there. Nicky—she didn't know—"

She could be so blanched and so stricken when the saga of her motherhood came out in her eyes, the pallor of her face jutting out her features like lonely landmarks on waste land, that her husband and her son had learned how to dread for her and spare her.

"Now, mother!" said Nicholas, and rose to stand behind her chair, holding her poor, quavering chin in the cup of his hand. "Come, one rainy Sunday is enough. Let's not have an indoor as well as an outdoor storm. Come along. Didn't I hear Miss Ada play the piano one evening over at Leo's? Up-see-la! Who said you weren't my favorite dancing partner?" and waltzed her, half dragging back, toward the parlor. "Come, some music!"

There were the usual demurrings from Ada, rather prettily pink, and Mrs. Turkletaub, with the threat of sobs swallowed, opening the upright piano to dust the dustless keyboard with her apron, and Nicholas, his sagging pipe quickly supplied with one of the rose-twined cuspidors for ash receiver, hunched down in the pink-velour armchair of enormous upholstered hips.

The "Turkish Patrol" was what Ada played, and then, "Who Is Sylvia?" and sang it, as fraily as a bird.

At one o'clock there was dinner, that immemorial Sunday meal of roast chicken with its supplicating legs up off the platter; dressing to be gouged out; sweet potatoes in amber icing; a master stroke of Mrs. Turkletaub's called "*matzos klose*," balls of unleavened bread, sizzling, even as she served them, in a hot butter bath and light-brown onions; a stuffed goose neck, bursting of flavor; cheese pie twice the depth of the fork that cut in; coffee in large cups. More cracking of nuts, interspersed with raisins. Ada, cunningly enveloped in a much-too-large apron, helping Mrs. Turkletaub to clear it all away.

Smoking there in his chair beside the dining-room window, rain the unrelenting threnody of the day, Nicholas, fed, closed his eyes to the rhythm of their comings and goings through the swinging door that led to the kitchen. Comings—and—goings—his mother who rustled so cleanly of starch—Ada—clear—yes, that was it—clear as a mountain stream. Their small laughters—comings—goings—

It was almost dusk when he awoke, the pink-shaded piano lamp already lighted in the parlor beyond, the window shade at his side drawn and an Afghan across his knees. It was snug there in the rosied dusk. The women were in the kitchen yet, or was it again? Again, he supposed, looking at his watch. He had slept three hours. Presently he rose and sauntered out. There was coffee fragrance on the air of the large white kitchen, his mother hunched to the attitude of wielding a can opener, and at the snowy oilclothed table, Ada, slicing creamy slabs off the end of a cube of Swiss cheese.

"Sleepyhead," she greeted, holding up a sliver for him to nibble.

And his mother: "That was a good rest for you, son? You feel better?"

"Immense," he said, hunching his shoulders and stretching his hands down into his pockets in a yawny well-being.

"I wish, then, you would put another leaf in the table for me. There's four besides your father coming over from Aunt Gussie's. I just wish you would look at Ada. For a girl that don't have to turn her hand at home, with two servants, and a laundress every other week, just look how handy she is with everything she touches."

The litter of Sunday-night supper, awaiting its transfer to the dining-room table, lay spread in the faithful geometry of the cold, hebdomadal repast. A platter of ruddy sliced tongue; one of noonday remnants of cold chicken; ovals of liverwurst; a mound of potato salad crisscrossed with strips of pimento; a china basket of the stuffed dates, all kissed with sugar; half of an enormously thick cheese cake; two uncovered apple pies; a stack of delicious raisin-stuffed curlicues, known as *"schneken,"* pickles with a fern of dill across them (Ada's touch, the dill); a dish of stuffed eggs with a toothpick stuck in each half (also Ada's touch, the toothpicks).

She moved rather pussily, he thought, sometimes her fair cheeks quivering slightly to the vibration of her walk, as if they had jelled. And, too, there was something rather snug and plump in the way her little hands with the eight dimples moved about things, laying the slabs of Swiss cheese, unstacking cups.

"No, only seven cups, Ada. Nicky—ain't going to be home to supper."

"Oh," she said, "excuse me! I—I—thought—silly—" and looked up at him to deny that it mattered.

"Isn't that what you said this morning, Nicky?" Poor Sara, she almost failed herself then because her voice ended in quite a dry click in her throat.

He stood watching the resumed unstacking of the cups, each with its crisp little grate against its neighbor.

"One," said Ada, "two-three-four-five-six—seven!"

He looked very long and lean and his darkly nervous self, except that he dilly-dallied on his heels like a much-too-tall boy not wanting to look foolish.

"If Miss Ada will provide another cup and saucer, I think I'll stay home."

"As you will," said Sara, disappearing into the dining room with the mound of salad and the basket of sugar-kissed dates.

She put them down rather hastily when she got there, because, sillily enough, she thought, for the merest instant, she was going to faint.

* * * * *

The week that Judge Turkletaub tried his first case in Court of General Sessions—a murder case, toward which his criminal-law predilection seemed so inevitably to lead him, his third child, a little daughter with lovely creamy skin against slightly too curly hair, was lying, just two days old, in a blue-and-white nursery with an absurd border of blue ducks waddling across the wallpaper.

Ada, therefore, was not present at this inaugural occasion of his first trial. But each of the two weeks of its duration, in a first-row bench of the privileged, so that her gaze was almost on a dotted line with her son's, sat Sara Turkletaub, her hands crossed over her waistline, her bosom filling and waning and the little jet folderols on her bonnet blinking. Tears had their way with her, prideful, joyful at her son's new estate, sometimes bitterly salt at the life in the naked his eyes must look upon.

Once, during the recital of the defendant, Sara almost seemed to bleed her tears, so poignantly terrible they came, scorching her eyes of a pain too exquisite to be analyzed, yet too excruciating to be endured.

III

Venture back, will you, to the ice and red of that Russian dawn when on the snow the footsteps that led toward the horizon were the color of blood, and one woman, who could not keep her eyes ahead, moaned as she fled, prayed, and even screamed to return to her dead in the bullet-riddled horse trough.

Toward the noon of that day, a gray one that smelled charred, a fugitive group from a distant village that was still burning faltered, as it too fled toward the horizon, in the blackened village of Vodna, because a litter had to be fashioned for an old man whose feet were frozen, and a mother, whose baby had perished at her breast, would bury her dead.

Huddled beside the horse trough, over a poor fire she had kindled of charred wood, Hanscha, the midwife (Hanscha, the drunk, they called her, fascinatedly, in the Pale of generations of sober women), spied Mosher's flung coat and reached for it eagerly, with an eye to tearing it into strips to wrap her tortured feet.

A child stirred as she snatched it, wailing lightly, and the instinct of her calling, the predominant motive, Hanscha with her fumy breath warmed it closer to life and trod the one hundred and eight miles to the port with it strapped to her back like a pack.

Thus it was that Schmulka, the red twin, came to America and for the first fourteen years of his life slept on a sour pallet in a sour tenement he shared with Hanscha, who with filthy hands brought children into the filthy slums.

Jason, she called him, because that was the name of the ship that carried them over. A rolling tub that had been horrible with the cries of cattle and seasickness.

At fourteen he was fierce and rebellious and down on the Juvenile Court records for truancy, petty trafficking in burned-out opium, vandalism, and gang vagrancy.

In Hanscha's sober hours he was her despair, and she could be horrible in her anger, once the court reprimanding her and threatening to take Jason from her because of welts found on his back.

It was in her cups that she was proud of him, and so it behooved Jason to drink her down to her pallet, which he could, easily.

He was handsome. His red hair had darkened to the same bronze of the samovar and he was straight as the drop of an apple from the branch. He was reckless. Could turn a pretty penny easily, even dangerously, and spend it with a flip for a pushcart bauble.

Once he brought home a plaster-of-Paris Venus—the Melos one with the beautiful arch to her torso of a bow that instant after the arrow has flown. Hanscha cuffed him for the expenditure, but secretly her old heart, which since childhood had subjected her to strange, rather epileptical, sinking spells, and had induced the drinking, warmed her with pride in his choice.

Hanscha, with her veiny nose and the dreadful single hair growing out of a mole on her chin, was not without her erudition. She had read for the midwifery, and back in the old days could recite the bones in the body.

She let the boy read nights, sometimes even to dropping another coin into the gas meter. Some of the books were the lewd penny ones of the Bowery bookstands, old medical treatises, too, purchased three for a quarter and none too nice reading for the growing boy. But there he had also found a *Les Miserables* and *The Confessions of St. Augustine*, which last, if he had known it, was a rare edition, but destined for the ash pit.

Once he read Hanscha a bit of poetry out of a furiously stained old volume of verse, so fragrantly beautiful, to him, this bit, that it wound around him like incense, the perfume of it going deeply and stinging his eyes to tears:

> Our birth is but a sleep and a forgetting!
> The soul that rises with us, our life's star,
> Hath had elsewhere its setting,
> And cometh from afar.
> Not in entire forgetfulness,
> And not in utter nakedness,
> But trailing clouds of glory do we come

From God, who is our home:
Heaven lies about us in our infancy.
Shades of the prison house begin to close
Upon the growing boy,
But he beholds the light, and whence it flows
He sees it in his joy;
The youth who daily farther, from the East
Must travel, still is Nature's priest,
And by the vision splendid
Is on his way attended;
At length the man perceives it die away,
And fade into the light of common day.

But Hanscha was drunk and threw some coffee-sopped bread at him, and so his foray into poetry ended in the slops of disgust.

A Miss Manners, a society social worker who taught poverty sweet forbearance every Tuesday from four until six, wore a forty-eight-diamond bar pin on her under bodice (on Tuesday from four until six), and whose gray-suède slippers were ever so slightly blackened from the tripping trip from front door to motor and back, took him up, as the saying is, and for two weeks Jason disported himself on the shorn lawns of the Manners summer place at Great Neck, where the surf creamed at the edge of the terrace and the smell of the sea set something beating against his spirit as if it had a thousand imprisoned wings.

There he developed quite a flair for the law books in Judge Manners's laddered library. Miss Manners found him there, reading, on stomach and elbows, his heels waving in the air.

Judge Manners talked with him and discovered a legal turn of mind, and there followed some veranda talk of educating and removing him from his environment. But that very afternoon Jason did a horrid thing. It was no more than he had seen about him all his life. Not as much. He kissed the little pig-tailed daughter of the laundress and pursued her as she ran shrieking to her mother's apron. That was all, but his defiant head and the laundress's chance knowledge of his Juvenile Court record did for him.

At six o'clock that evening, with a five-dollar bill of which he made a spitball for the judge's departing figure down the station platform, he was shipped back to Hanscha. Secretly he was relieved. Life was easier in the tenement under the shadow of Brooklyn Bridge. The piece of its arch which he could see from his window was even beautiful, a curve of a stone into some beyond.

That night he fitted down into the mold his body had worn on the pallet, sighing out satisfaction.

Environment had won him back.

On the other hand, in one of those red star-spangled passions of rebellion against his fetid days, he blindly cut Hanscha with the edge of a book which struck against her brow as he hurled it. She had been drunk and had asked of him, at sixteen, because of the handsomeness that women would easily love in him, to cadet the neighborhood of Grand Street, using her tenement as his refuge of vice and herself as sharer of spoils.

The corner of the book cut deeply and pride in her terror of him came out redly in her bloodshot eyes.

In the short half term of his high-school training he had already forged ahead of his class when he attained the maturity of working papers. He was plunging eagerly—brilliantly, in fact—into a rapid translation of the *Iliad*, fired from the very first line by the epic of the hexametered anger of Achilles, and stubbornly he held out against the working papers.

But to Hanscha they came with the inevitability of a summons rather than an alternative, and so for a year or two he brought home rather precocious wages from his speed in a canning factory. Then he stoked his way to Sydney and back, returning fiery with new and terrible oaths.

One night Hanscha died. He found her crumpled up in the huddle of her skirts as if she had dropped in her tracks, which she had, in one of the epileptic heart strictures.

It was hardly a grief to him. He had seen red with passion at her atrociousness too often, and, somehow, everything that she stood for had been part of the ache in him.

Yet it is doubtful if, released of her, he found better pasture. Bigger pastures, it is true, in what might be called an upper stratum of the lower East Side, although at no time was he ever to become party to any of its underground system of crime.

Inevitably, the challenge of his personality cleared the way for him. At nineteen he had won and lost the small fortune of thirty-three hundred dollars at a third-class gambling resort where he came in time to be croupier.

He dressed flashily, wore soft collars, was constantly swapping sporty scarfpins for sportier ones, and was inevitably the center, seldom part, of a group.

Then one evening at Cooper Union, which stands at the head of the Bowery, he enrolled for an evening course in law, but never entered the place again.

Because the next night, in a Fourteenth Street cabaret with adjacent gambling rooms, he met one who called herself Winnie Ross, the beginning of a heart-sickening end.

There is so little about her to relate. She was the color of cloyed honey when the sugar granules begin to show through. Pale, pimply in a fashion the powder could cover up, the sag of her facial muscles showed plainly through, as if weary of doling out to the years their hush money, and she was quite obviously down at the heels. Literally so, because when she took them off, her shoes lopped to the sides and could not stand for tipsiness.

She was Jason's first woman. She exhaled a perfume, cheap, tickling, chewed some advertised tablets that scented her kisses, and her throat, when she threw up her head, had an arch and flex to it that were mysteriously graceful.

Life had been swift and sheer with Winnie. She was very tired and, paradoxically enough, it gave her one of her last remaining charms. Her eyelids were freighted with weariness, were waxy white of it, and they could flutter to her cheeks, like white butterflies against white, and lay shadows there that maddened Jason.

She called him Red, although all that remained now were the lights through his browning hair, almost like the flashings of a lantern down a railroad track.

She pronounced it with a slight trilling of the R, and if it was left in her of half a hundred loves to stir on this swift descent of her life line, she did over Jason. Partly because he was his winged-Hermes self, and partly because—because—it was difficult for her rather fagged brain to rummage back.

Thus the rest may be told:

Entering her rooms one morning, a pair of furiously garish ones over a musical-instrument store on the Bowery, he threw himself full length on the red-cotton divan, arms locked under his always angry-looking head, and watching her, through low lids, trail about the room at the business of preparing him a surlily demanded cup of coffee. Her none too immaculate pink robe trailed a cotton-lace tail irritatingly about her heels, which slip-slopped as she walked, her stockings, without benefit of support, twisting about her ankles.

She was barometer for his moods, which were elemental, and had learned to tremble with a queer exaltation of fear before them.

"My Red-boy blue to-day," she said, stooping as she passed and wanting to kiss him.

He let his lids drop and would have none of her. They were curiously blue, she thought, as if of unutterable fatigue, and then quickly appraised that his luck was still letting him in for the walloping now of two weeks' duration. His diamond-and-opal scarfpin was gone, and the gold cuff links replaced with mother-of-pearl.

She could be violently bitter about money, and when the flame of his personality was not there to be reckoned with, ten times a day she ejected him, with a venom that was a psychosis, out of her further toleration. Not so far gone was Winnie but that she could count on the twist of her body and the arch of her throat as revenue getters.

At first Jason had been lavish, almost with a smack of some of the old days she had known, spending with the easy prodigality of the gambler in luck. There was a near-seal coat from him in her cupboard of near-silks, and the flimsy wooden walls of her rooms had been freshly papered in roses.

Then his luck had turned, and to top his sparseness with her this new sullenness which she feared and yet which could be so delicious to her— reminiscently delicious.

She gave him coffee, and he drank it like medicine out of a thick-lipped cup painted in roses.

"My Red-boy blue," she reiterated, trying to ingratiate her arms about his neck. "Red-boy tells Winnie he won't be back for two whole days and then brings her surprise party very next day. Red-boy can't stay away from Winnie."

"Let go."

"Red-boy bring Winnie nothing? Not little weeny, weeny nothing?" drawing a design down his coat sleeve, her mouth bunched.

Suddenly he jerked her so that the breath jumped in a warm fan of it against her face.

"You're the only thing I've got in the world, Win. My luck's gone, but I've got you. Tell me I've got you."

He could be equally intense over which street car to take, and she knew it, but somehow it lessened for her none of the lure of his nervosity, and with her mind recoiling from his pennilessness her body inclined.

"Tell me, Winnie, that I have you."

"You know you have," she said, and smiled, with her head back so that her face foreshortened.

"I'm going far for you Winnie. Gambling is too rotten—and too easy. I want to build bridges for you. Practice law. Corner Wall Street."

This last clicked.

"Once," she said, lying back, with her pupils enlarging with the fleeting memories she was not always alert enough to clutch—"once—once when I lived around Central Park—a friend of mine—vice-president he was—Well, never mind, he was my friend—it was nothing for him to turn over a thousand or two a week for me in Wall Street."

This exaggeration was gross, but it could feed the flame of his passion for her like oil.

"I'll work us up and out of this! I've got better stuff in me. I want to wind you in pearls—diamonds—sapphires."

"I had a five-thousand-dollar string once—of star sapphires."

"Trust me, Winnie. Help me by having confidence in me. I'm glad my luck is welching. It will be lean at first, until I get on my legs. But it's not too late yet. Win, if only I have some one to stand by me. To believe—to fight with and for me! Get me, girl? Believe in me."

"Sure. Always play strong with the cops, Red. It's the short cut to ready money. Ready money, Red. That's what gets you there. Don't ask any girl to hang on if it's shy. That's where I spun myself dirt many a time, hanging on after it got shy. Ugh! That's what did for me—hanging on—after it got shy."

"No. No. You don't understand. For God's sake try to get me, Winnie. Fight up with me. It'll be lean, starting, but I'll finish strong for you."

"Don't lean on me. I'm no wailing wall. What's it to me all your highfaluting talk. You've been as slab-sided in the pockets as a cat all month. Don't have to stand it. I've got friends—spenders—"

There had been atrocious scenes, based on his jealousies of her, which some imp in her would lead her to provoke, notwithstanding that even as she spoke she regretted, and reached back for the words,

"I mean—"

"I know what you mean," he said, quietly, permitting her to lie back against him and baring his teeth down at her.

She actually thought he was smiling.

"I'm not a dead one by a long shot," she said, kindling with what was probably her desire to excite him.

"No?"

"No. I can still have the best. The very best. If you want to know it, a political Indian with a car as long as this room, not mentioning any names, is after me—"

She still harbored the unfortunate delusion that he was smiling.

"You thought I was up at Ossining this morning, didn't you?" he asked, lazily for him. He went there occasionally to visit a friend in the state prison who had once served him well in a gambling raid and was now doing a short larceny term there.

"You said you were—"

"I *said* I was. Yes. But I came back unexpectedly, didn't I?"

"Y-yes, Red?"

"Look at me!"

She raised round and ready-to-be-terrified eyes.

"Murphy was here last night!" he cracked at her, bang-bang-bang-bang-bang, like so many pistol shots.

"Why, Red—I—You—"

"Don't lie. Murphy was here last night! I saw him leave this morning as I came in."

It was hazard, pure and simple. Not even a wild one, because all too easily he could kiss down what would be sure to be only her half-flattered resentment.

But there was a cigar stub on the table edge, and certain of her adjustments of the room when he entered had been rather quick. He could be like that with her, crazily the slave of who knows what beauty he found in her; jealous of even an unaccountable inflection in her voice. There had been unmentionable frenzies of elemental anger between them and she feared and exulted in these strange poles of his nature.

"Murphy was here last night!"

It had happened, in spite of a caution worthy of a finer finesse than hers, and suddenly she seemed to realize the quality of her fear for him to whom she was everything and who to her was not all.

"Don't, Red," she said, all the bars of her pretense down and dodging from his eyes rather than from any move he made toward her. "Don't, Red. Don't!" And began to whimper in the unbeautifulness of fear, becoming strangely smaller as her pallor mounted.

He was as terrible and as swarthy and as melodramatic as Othello.

"Don't, Red," she called still again, and it was as if her voice came to him from across a bog.

He was standing with one knee dug into the couch, straining her head back against the wall, his hand on her forehead and the beautiful flexing arch of her neck rising … swanlike.

"Watch out!" There was a raw nail in the wall where a picture had hung. Murphy had kept knocking it awry and she had removed it. "Watch out, Red! No-o—no—"

Through the star-spangled red he glimpsed her once where the hair swept off her brow, and for the moment, to his blurred craziness, it was as if through the red her brow was shotted with little scars and pock marks from glass, and a hot surge of unaccountable sickness fanned the enormous silence of his rage.

With or without his knowing it, that raw nail drove slowly home to the rear of Winnie's left ear, upward toward the cerebellum as he tilted and tilted, and the convex curve of her neck mounted like a bow stretched outward.

* * * * *

There was little about Jason's trial to entitle it to more than a back-page paragraph in the dailies. He sat through those days, that were crisscrossed with prison bars, much like those drowned figures encountered by deep-sea divers, which, seated upright in death, are pressed down by the waters of unreality.

It is doubtful if he spoke a hundred words during the lean, celled weeks of his waiting, and then with a vacuous sort of apathy and solely upon advice of counsel. Even when he took the stand, undramatically, his voice, without even a plating of zest for life, was like some old drum with the parchment too tired to vibrate.

Women, however, cried over him and the storm in his eyes and the curiously downy back of his neck where the last of his youth still marked him.

To Sara, from her place in the first row, on those not infrequent occasions when his eyes fumbled for hers, he seemed to drown in her gaze—back—somewhere—

On a Friday at high noon the jury adjourned, the judge charging it with a solemnity that rang up to wise old rafters and down into one woman's thirsty soul like life-giving waters.

In part he told the twelve men about to file out, "If there has been anything in my attitude during the recital of the defendant's story, which has appeared to you to be in the slightest manner prejudiced one way or another, I charge you to strike such mistaken impressions from your minds.

"I have tried honestly to wash the slate of my mind clean to take down faithfully the aspects of this case which for two weeks has occupied this jury.

"If you believe the defendant guilty of the heinous crime in question, do not falter in your use of the power with which the law has vested you.

"If, on the other hand and to the best of your judgment, there has been in the defendant's life extenuating circumstances, er—a limitation of environment, home influence, close not the avenues of your fair judgment.

"Did this man in the kind of er—a—frenzy he describes and to which witnesses agree he was subject, deliberately strain back the Ross woman's head until the nail penetrated?

"If so, remember the law takes knowledge only of self-defense.

"On the other hand, ask of yourselves well, did the defendant, in the frenzy which he claims had hold of him when he committed this unusual crime, know that the nail was there?

"*Would Winnie Ross have met her death if the nail had not been there?*

"Gentlemen, in the name of the law, solemnly and with a fear of God in your hearts, I charge you."

It was a quick verdict. Three hours and forty minutes.

"Not guilty."

In the front row there, with the titillating folderols on her bonnet and her hand at her throat as if she would tear it open for the mystery of the pain of the heartbeat in it, Sara Turkletaub heard, and, hearing, swooned into the pit of her pain and her joy.

Her son, with brackets of fatigue out about his mouth, was standing over her when she opened her eyes, the look of crucifixion close to the front of them.

"Mother," he said, pressing her head close to his robes of state and holding a throat-straining quiver under his voice, "I—I shouldn't have let you stay. It was too—much for you."

It took her a moment for the mist to clear.

"I—Son—did somebody strike? Hit? Strange. I—I must have been hurt. Son, am I bleeding?" And looked down, clasping her hand to the bosom of her decent black-silk basque.

"Son, I—It was a good verdict, not? I—couldn't have stood it—if—if it wasn't. I—Something—It was good, not?"

"Yes, mother, yes."

"Don't—don't let that boy get away, son. I think—those tempers—I can help—him. You see, I know—how to handle—Somehow I—"

"Yes, mother, only now you must sit quietly—"

"Promise me, son, you won't let him get away without I see him?"

"Yes, dear, only please now—a moment—quiet—"

You see, the judge was very tired, and, looking down at the spot where her hand still lay at her bosom as if to press down a hurt, the red of her same obsession shook and shook him.

Somehow it seemed to him, too, that her dear heart was bleeding.

THE END

Milton Keynes UK
Ingram Content Group UK Ltd.
UKHW030838021124
450589UK00006B/704